AUCKLAND

ANDREW HEMPSTEAD

Contents

Waikato, Coromandel, and the Bay of Plenty.......... 88

AUCKLAND

AUCKLAND

Auckland has always offered wonderful scenery, and in the last decade an incredible energy has been injected into almost every corner of city, transforming this cosmopolitan center of 1.3 million into a world-class tourist destination. Most international visitors touch down in Auckland, but the city has grown into a lot more than simply a gateway to the rest of the country. It's a vibrant, exciting city, with a mix of attractions to suit both outdoor enthusiasts and those who thrive in a bustling concrete-and-glass metropolis.

Straddling a narrow piece of land between magnificent Waitemata and Manukau Harbours, Auckland is flanked by the South Pacific Ocean to the east and the Tasman Sea to the west. The downtown area slopes to Waitemata Harbour, which is dotted with boats of all kinds, the water a sparkling backdrop to many colorful sails. Nicknamed the "City of Sails," Auckland has hosted the America's Cup on two occasions in the last decade. It was these races that set in motion a downtown harborfront rejuvenation that is the envy of cities the world over.

Auckland is also known for its many fine beaches, beautiful parks and gardens, and a great variety of restaurants and nightlife. The city's eastern shoreline offers calm water and protected beaches, while the western shores boast wild waves, good surfing, and desolate windswept beaches. The urban area is wrapped around a number of extinct volcanic

© ANDREW HEMPSTEAD

HIGHLIGHTS

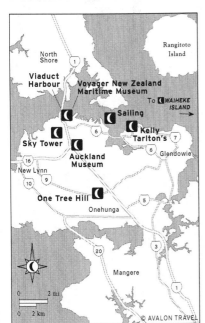

(Voyager New Zealand Maritime Museum: Learn about Auckland's long association with the ocean, from the arrival of the first Maori to the America's Cup (page 12).

(Viaduct Harbour: Developed for the America's Cup, this waterfront precinct has matured into a stylish mix of restaurants and shops (page 14).

(Auckland Museum: Maori culture, natural history, and the story of Auckland are all under one roof in the imposing museum within the Auckland Domain (page 16).

(Kelly Tarlton's: Dedicated to the wonders of the ocean, this underground attraction is a good way to get a taste for the marinelife you'll experience beyond city limits (page 17).

(One Tree Hill: Walk or drive to the top of this dormant volcano, an oasis of green surrounded by suburbia (watch for grazing sheep), and immerse yourself in Maori history while enjoying sweeping city views (page 19).

(Sailing: Known as the "City of Sails," Auckland is the perfect place to try your hand at sailing, with charter yachts lining up at Viaduct Harbour for your business (page 21).

(Waiheke Island: Easily reached by ferry from downtown, this island boasts a beautiful year-round climate, secluded beaches, wineries, and many boutique accommodations (page 44).

LOOK FOR (TO FIND RECOMMENDED SIGHTS, ACTIVITIES, DINING, AND LODGING.

(Sky Tower: Take a ride to the top of this landmark high above the city for spectacular views of the skyline and harbor (page 12).

peaks that host vantage points with great views. From these scattered lookouts, you can see how Auckland has also been developed around parks and gardens—packed on weekends with walkers, joggers, cricketers, kite enthusiasts, and families enjoying the year-round pleasant climate (summer average is 23°C/73°F; winter average is a balmy 14°C/57°F).

Within sight of downtown, the 47 islands of Hauraki Gulf Maritime Park beckon. The park is accessed by ferry from downtown; a day trip

will give you a taste of island life, but beautiful beaches, upscale lodgings, and world-class wineries make an overnight trip tempting.

Auckland has evolved into one of the world's most tourist-friendly cities. Budget travelers will be amazed by the high standard of inner-city backpacker lodges complete with rooftop hot tubs, while those with more money to spend can relax in one of the world's most perfectly placed Hilton hotels. The coffee in Auckland is equally impressive, with all sorts

AUCKLAND

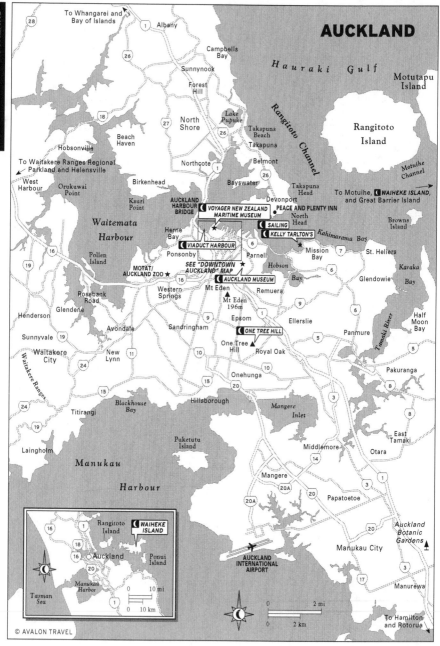

of wonderful caffeine brews equal in quality to those in any place I've ever been. Auckland's better restaurants bring together the country's finest game and produce (and wine) for a dining experience that can run into hundreds of dollars (or under $5 for a gourmet pie from Pie Mania). To ensure your stay is as easy and worthwhile as possible, visitor centers dot the city, where staff hand out free information and make transportation and accommodation bookings at no charge.

PLANNING YOUR TIME

Most visitors to New Zealand land in Auckland at the end of a long flight. Therefore, I highly recommend you plan on spending the first night in Auckland, giving you time to acclimatize, to recover from any jet lag, and simply to spend the first day without having to "travel." Even the most free-spirited travelers will know in advance which day they will be arriving, so even if

the schedule for the rest of your vacation is flexible, reserve accommodations for the first night before leaving home. With the same thought in mind, also make reservations for the night before your departure. For those not staying in backpacker lodges, I'd recommend staying at a downtown hotel upon arrival (close to major attractions and not a culture shock) and a bed-and-breakfast with character to finish your New Zealand journey. This also gives you a couple of nights to savor the city's many restaurants; be sure to enjoy a waterfront dining experience.

Once the practical aspects of your stay have been organized, you can start to figure out what you want to see and what isn't so important. Obviously this has a lot to do with personal tastes, but I highly recommend everyone start from the top—literally—by riding the elevator up the **Sky Tower** to the top of New Zealand's highest building. Back at ground level, it's a short walk down to the harbor and the **Voyager**

© ANDREW HEMPSTEAD

Auckland Museum

New Zealand Maritime Museum and adjacent **Viaduct Harbour,** both of which give great insight into the city's nautical flavor (as do the restaurants around Viaduct Harbour, a great lunchtime stop if you started early). With only one full day in Auckland, you could spend the afternoon at either the **Auckland Museum,** to learn about the region's natural and human history, or **Kelly Tarlton's,** to immerse yourself in the country's marinelife.

If, as I suggested earlier, you spend one night in Auckland at either end of your New Zealand trip, you could mix the above itinerary around to spend a rainy day indoors, leaving Sky Tower and the harbor for a sunny (or "fine," as they say locally) day. A fine day is also the time to travel beyond downtown to reach the low summit of **One Tree Hill,** one of many volcanic peaks within city limits.

The ocean should be incorporated somewhere into your Auckland stay, and I don't mean simply sipping a cocktail at a harborfront bar. Jumping aboard a ferry is an easy and inexpensive way to see the city from water level, but a better way is to go **sailing** on one of the charter yachts that tie up at Viaduct Harbour.

If you have three full days in Auckland, allow yourself at least one day to visit Hauraki Gulf Maritime Park, where **Waiheke Island** and its beautiful beaches and scenic wineries are linked to downtown by ferry.

Sights

While New Zealand's largest city is filled with official attractions that you won't want to miss, there are also parks and gardens to explore, a magnificent harborfront, and many interesting suburbs. Offshore lies an archipelago of islands, easily reached as a day trip from downtown.

DOWNTOWN

Queen Street is downtown Auckland's main commercial corridor, and many attractions are within walking distance. Sky Tower is a good starting point, both for its sweeping city views and as home to the main information center. Combine the Sky Tower with harborside attractions and the art gallery, both easily reached on foot, and you will have already filled one day of sightseeing.

◖ Sky Tower

For excellent views of Auckland from the Southern Hemisphere's tallest building, head to the distinctive 328-meter (1,076-foot) Sky Tower (Victoria St., 09/363-6000; daily 8:30 A.M.–11 P.M.; adult $28, child $11). From the SkyCity casino at street level, three glass-fronted elevators whisk visitors to four observation decks in just 40 seconds. Make the Main Observation Level your first destination here; glass floor panels allow views of the city streets directly below and live weather reports flash on a screen. The highest point with public access is Skydeck, an outdoor viewing platform. Below the main deck is Sky Lounge. Before heading up Sky Tower, you can watch a documentary on the city's history.

The high-adrenaline activities for which New Zealand is so well known start right here in Auckland. **Sky Jump** (09/368-1835 or 0800/759-586; daily 10 A.M.–6 P.M.; $225) is a bungy-type setup 192 meters (630 ft) up Sky Tower. Rather than rebounding, jumpers wrapped in a body harness come to a smooth stop a few meters above a street-side platform.

◖ Voyager New Zealand Maritime Museum

On Hobson Wharf at the west end of Quay Street, this museum (09/373-0800; Oct.–Apr.

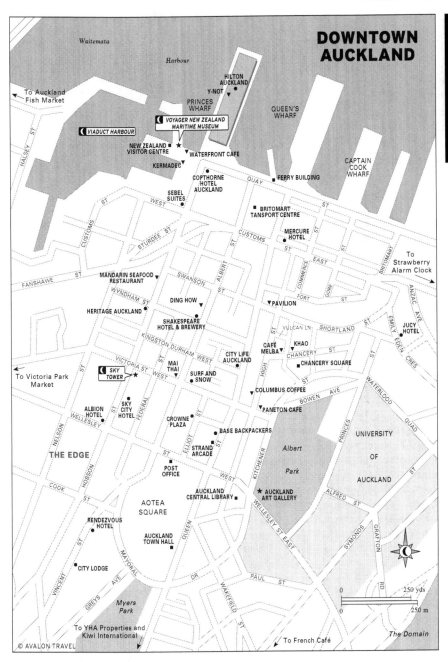

DOWNTOWN AUCKLAND

Waitemata

Harbour

HILTON AUCKLAND
Y-NOT

PRINCES WHARF

QUEEN'S WHARF

← To Auckland Fish Market

VOYAGER NEW ZEALAND MARITIME MUSEUM

VIADUCT HARBOUR

NEW ZEALAND VISITOR CENTRE ★

WATERFRONT CAFE

KERMADEC

CAPTAIN COOK WHARF

COPTHORNE HOTEL AUCKLAND

QUAY

FERRY BUILDING

SEBEL SUITES

HALSEY ST

CUSTOMS ST

WEST ST

BRITOMART TANSPORT CENTRE

STURDEE ST

CUSTOMS

MERCURE HOTEL

EAST ST

To Strawberry Alarm Clock

FANSHAWE ST

MANDARIN SEAFOOD RESTAURANT

SWANSON

ALBERT ST

COMMERCE ST

GORE ST

ANZAC AVE

WYNDHAM ST

DING HOW

PAVILION

FORT ST

EMILY EDEN CRES

JUCY HOTEL

HERITAGE AUCKLAND

SHAKESPEARE HOTEL & BREWERY

KINGSTON

DURHAM WEST

VULCAN LN

SHORTLAND ST

CITY LIFE AUCKLAND

CAFÉ MELBA

KHAO

CHANCERY

CHANCERY SQUARE

VICTORIA ST

MAI THAI

WEST ST

SURF AND SNOW

HIGH ST

COLUMBUS COFFEE

WATERLOO QUAD

SKY TOWER ★

BOWEN AVE

← To Victoria Park Market

PANETON CAFE

PRINCES ST

UNIVERSITY

ALBION HOTEL

SKY CITY HOTEL

FEDERAL ST

CROWNE PLAZA

BASE BACKPACKERS

NELSON ST

WELLESLEY ST

THE EDGE

ELLIOT ST

STRAND ARCADE

Albert

OF

HOBSON ST

COOK ST

POST OFFICE

WEST

KITCHENER ST

Park

AUCKLAND

ALFRED ST

SYMONDS ST

GRAFTON RD

AUCKLAND CENTRAL LIBRARY

AUCKLAND ART GALLERY ★

WELLESLEY ST EAST

AOTEA SQUARE

RENDEZVOUS HOTEL

AUCKLAND TOWN HALL

QUEEN ST

VINCENT ST

CITY LODGE

MAYORAL DR

PAUL ST

GREYS AVE

Myers Park

WAKEFIELD ST

0   250 yds

0   250 m

To YHA Properties and Kiwi International

To French Café

The Domain

© AVALON TRAVEL

QUEEN STREET

Downtown's main commercial thoroughfare, Queen Street, stretches from **Waitemata Harbour** as far south as suburban Newton. This busy cosmopolitan strip bustles with businesspeople, shoppers, and tourists. On weekends it's decisively quieter, with Aucklanders preferring nearby parks and beaches.

At the harbor end, the **Ferry Building** is the departure point for ferries to the North Shore and offshore islands. Across Quay Street, the old post office has been transformed into **Britomart Transport Centre,** a transportation interchange for buses and trains. From this point, Queen Street begins its long uphill journey. Street level at the bottom end is lined with tourist-oriented businesses, such as duty-free shopping and currency exchange outlets, as well as cafés and restaurants.

A few blocks up from the harbor, **The Edge** precinct is a combination of old and modern centered around a busy square surrounded by the town hall and various entertainment venues.

Toward the upper end, Queen Street crosses Karangahape Road, nicknamed **"K Road."** This area has a bustling Polynesian atmosphere and a variety of foreign nationalities represented in the shops, restaurants, and takeaway food stands.

© ANDREW HEMPSTEAD

Auckland Town Hall

daily 9 A.M.–6 P.M., rest of year 9 A.M.–5 P.M.; adult $17, senior $14, child $9) showcases New Zealand's strong maritime traditions in more than a dozen galleries—from the earliest craft used by Pacific Islanders to the latest technology used in the America's Cup. The museum encompasses a floating boatshed where traditional Maori crafts are displayed and visitors can try their hand at rowing. Other galleries feature hands-on displays, local lighthouses, an audiovisual presentation in the Pacific Discovery Theatre, a collection of canoes, boatbuilding workshops, and Black Magic, which tells the story of legendary New Zealand skipper Peter Blake. A number of historic craft are tied alongside the museum, and one of them, a small steamboat (with museum admission

adult $29, senior $24, child $14.50), takes visitors around the dock area.

Viaduct Harbour

Immediately west of the maritime museum is Viaduct Harbour (also known as **Viaduct Basin**), developed in the 1990s for Auckland's hosting of the America's Cup. A variety of venues around Hauraki Gulf were considered for the occasion, including offshore islands, but this downtown location was the final choice for the America's Cup village, breathing new life into a run-down commercial and industrial area that was first used as a port in the 1870s. Today, the harbor is filled with leisure craft and charter boats while the surrounding space holds a variety of restaurants and bars.

A pedestrian bridge crosses the harbor, leading to the architecturally impressive Viaduct Events Centre (where an outside promenade allows for good views back across the harbor to downtown), the Auckland Fish Market, and a number of warehouses that have been converted into restaurants.

Beyond the restaurants is the **North Wharf** precinct, with an ocean-inspired playground and multistory viewing platforms that allow a great view across working shipyards.

The Edge

A few blocks up from the harbor and immediately south of Wellesley Street, The Edge is a bustling precinct that centers around **Aotea Square.** The square is a popular city gathering place, filled with gardens and host to markets every Friday and Saturday. The **Civic** (corner of Queen and Wellesley Streets) opened in 1929 as a movie palace but fell into disrepair over time. After extensive renovations it reopened in 1999, restored to its former Asian-influenced art nouveau glory. In addition to showing films, the Civic hosts touring musicals and shows.

Across Aotea Square from the Civic, **Auckland Town Hall** is an Italian Renaissance–style building that dates to 1911. Like the Civic, it has undergone extensive renovations and is now home to the New Zealand Symphony Orchestra and Auckland Philharmonic Orchestra; the companies take advantage of the renowned acoustics of the Great Hall and Concert Chamber, respectively. Take in a performance by one of these two companies to experience the town hall in its best light, or wander through the public areas daily 9 A.M.–5 P.M.

A modern addition to The Edge, the **Aotea Centre** is a multipurpose venue that includes two major theaters and the country's largest convention center.

Auckland Art Gallery

Two blocks from Queen Street is the Auckland

© ANDREW HEMPSTEAD

Sky Tower

Art Gallery (corner of Lorne and Wellesley Streets, 09/379-1349; daily 10 A.M.–5 P.M.; free), which dates to 1888 and is the oldest and largest gallery in the country. Reopened in late 2011 after major renovations, the gallery displays an extensive historic and contemporary New Zealand art collection, as well as British and old master paintings, and a drawing and print collection. Free guided tours depart daily at 2 P.M. from the front desk. There's also a café, open daily for breakfast and lunch, and a gift shop.

Albert Park

When visiting the Auckland Art Gallery, take time to stroll through the Victorian-style gardens of this city park, admiring the groves of well-established oak trees, delightful fountains, and a historic rotunda. At the top end of the park is an old caretaker's cottage (daily 10 A.M.–4 P.M.), which now houses a collection of clocks from around the world.

© ANDREW HEMPSTEAD

Viaduct Harbour

THE DOMAIN

Auckland Domain is a large, lush, shady park within walking distance of both the city center and Parnell area. Covering more than 80 hectares, the park offers the Auckland Museum, Wintergarden, Fernz Fernery, Planetarium, and Herb Garden, a kiosk selling drinks and ice cream, and a restaurant that's a favorite spot for wedding receptions. On the hillsides, particularly outside the museum, kite-flying is popular—on a bright summer day the sky is alive with color and movement.

The beautiful **Wintergarden** (daily 10 A.M.–4 P.M.; free) is a short stroll from the museum. Flower gardens, several greenhouses with amazing hothouse plants, a lily pond, and shady courtyards with statue-lined footpaths make this a relaxing spot to hang out. A small lake, home to a flock of greedy ducks, makes it a popular place with bread-toting children. **Fernz Fernery** (daily 10 A.M.–4 P.M.; free), beside the Wintergarden, was originally a quarry.

Today, more than 150 varieties of fern thrive in three distinct zones—dry, intermediate, and wet—creating a stunning collection of species found in all parts of the country.

◖ Auckland Museum

Built on the highest point of the Domain, the Auckland Museum (Domain Dr., 09/309-0443; daily 10 A.M.–5 P.M.; adult $10, child free) boasts terrific views of Waitemata Harbour, Rangitoto Island, and the North Shore from the steps leading up to its impressive entrance. Inside is one of the best collections of Maori art and artifacts. Several floors feature a large variety of both permanent and changing exhibitions: the Hall of Pacific Art contains art and objects from islands throughout the Pacific; another exhibit explores Auckland's fascinating volcanic history, complete with sound effects and audiovisuals; other halls feature New Zealand's natural history, birdlife, ceramics, English furniture, military and maritime history, and Asian arts. You can lose complete track of time here—it's a good spot to keep in mind for a Sunday, when many attractions are closed, or for a rainy day. There's also a small coffee lounge and a good selection of Maori carvings, jewelry, books on New Zealand, and souvenirs available at average Auckland prices in the museum shop. For an introduction to Maori culture, attend one of the short tours of the Maori foyer with a traditional greeting, then a Maori Concert Party performance in the small auditorium at either 11:15 A.M. or 1:30 P.M. If you're driving, Maunsell Road provides access to a large parking lot ($5 per hour, or $7 per day if entering before 9 A.M.).

PARNELL

Parnell is Auckland's oldest suburb, located immediately east of The Domain. Today, it's a trendy little spot with chic shops, historic buildings, little cafés in shady arcades, a range of

© ANDREW HEMPSTEAD

Parnell Rose Gardens are an enjoyable free attraction east of downtown.

accommodations, and trendy restaurants by the handful.

Parnell is a gentle uphill walk from downtown—walk along Customs Street E (at the harbor end of Queen St.), curve left onto Beach Road, pass the railway station, and make a left on Parnell Rise, which becomes Parnell Road. East of Parnell Road is **Parnell Rose Gardens** (Gladstone Rd.; free), containing more than 4,000 roses.

Historic Parnell

The city's oldest building on its original site in Auckland is **Hulme Court** (350 Parnell Rd.), dating to 1843, but it is not open to the public. Instead, continue up Parnell Road to **St. Mary's Holy Trinity Cathedral** (420 Parnell Rd.), a wooden church dating to 1897, and then to the corner of St. Stephens Avenue, where the wooden buildings of **Bishop's Court** date to the 1860s.

Continue up Parnell Road and you soon reach **Kinder House** (2 Ayr St.). Built from Rangitoto Island volcanic stone and completed in 1857, it contains Georgian furniture, family heirlooms, and a collection of Rev. John Kinder's pioneer photographs taken between 1860 and 1888. Leave your vehicle at Kinder House and walk down the hill to **Ewelme Cottage** (14 Ayr St., 09/379-0202; Sun. 10:30 A.M.–4:30 P.M.; adult $8.50, child $3). Constructed of kauri, New Zealand's native timber, it is one of Parnell's many buildings preserved by the New Zealand Historic Places Trust.

EAST OF DOWNTOWN

Take Quay Street east from downtown and you will quickly find yourself on a causeway across the head of Hobson Bay. From here, Tamaki Drive hugs the shoreline and passes Kelly Tarlton's before rounding Bastion Point to reach the leafy suburb of Mission Bay, where cafés and boutiques line the busy main street. It's a pleasant drive or cycle, although it gets busy during rush hour.

◖ Kelly Tarlton's

New Zealander Kelly Tarlton, one of the world's premier underwater adventurers, spent most of his life traveling the world recovering lost treasures before developing this unique aquarium in underground storm-water holding tanks on Auckland's harbor (Tamaki Dr., 09/528-0603; daily 9:30 A.M.–5:30 P.M.; adult $34, senior $26, child $16) six km (3.7 mi) east from downtown. In 1994, eight years after Tarlton's untimely death (he died soon after the complex opened and never saw his dream fulfilled), the second stage of the project opened—a simulation of an Antarctic environment, including penguins. The journey begins by walking through a life-size replica of Captain Robert Scott's hut, complete with groaning ice and fierce winds. Then it's all aboard a Snow Cat that heads through an

© ANDREW HEMPSTEAD

Kinder House in Parnell

Antarctic whiteout, under the ice, past some penguins, and into a futuristic Scott Base. The second part of the complex is the aquarium. Travel on a moving walkway through a crystal-clear acrylic tunnel and step off at any point onto the footpath running alongside. Other than the walkway beneath your feet you're surrounded by water—all sorts of indigenous New Zealand sea creatures skim past the tunnel around you, while eels and crayfish peek out of rock crevices. The lighting, dark blue carpeting, and sound effects add to the submarine atmosphere. The tunnel darkens as you enter the deep-sea area, where sharks, stingrays, and other exotic creatures glide above and around you. In the small theater to the left of the main entrance room, an excellent audiovisual slide show features underwater photography; it's 10 minutes long and is shown every 15 minutes. Displays of shells and sea urchins and other objects of marine interest, a piranha tank (feeding time 11 A.M.) and touch tank, a souvenir shop,

and lots of articles about sharks complete this Auckland attraction.

WEST OF DOWNTOWN
Ponsonby
A fashionable suburb within walking distance from K Road, Ponsonby boasts many old homes and shops that have been beautifully restored. Entirely preserved Renall Street depicts a slice of 19th-century Auckland. Houses sit close together on the narrow and steep street, each house with a view of the harbor over the rooftops. Ponsonby is also known for its gourmet restaurants, intriguing shops, and trendy people. Buses run here from Queen Elizabeth Square past Victoria Park and College Hill. Get off at the Three Lamps stop; Renall Street is one block north.

MOTAT
In Western Springs, four km (2.5 mi) west of downtown, the **Museum of Transport and Technology** (Great North Rd., 09/815-5800; daily 10 A.M.–5 P.M.; adult $14, senior and child $8) is commonly referred to by its acronym, MOTAT. At the site of Auckland's original water source, MOTAT gives a glimpse into New Zealand's past with exhibitions of early agricultural machinery, airplanes, vintage cars, fire and steam engines, and a pioneer village. The aviation building is a flying buff's delight, with an extensive historical display featuring Richard Pearse, a South Island farmer and inventor who it's claimed made several flights in the summer of 1902, predating the Wright Brothers' 1903 exploits by over a year. Children will love the Tactile Dome, which is filled with interactive exhibits, including an earthquake simulator.

Auckland Zoo
Located in Western Springs, the zoo (Motions Rd., 09/360-3800; daily 9:30 A.M.–5:30 P.M.; adult $22, senior $18, child $11) contains 500

exotic and indigenous animals in enclosures such as Pridelands, which is home to a variety of African species. One of the highlights is the nocturnal house, where you can see the curious kiwi (native bird and a national symbol) doing his (or her) thing during the daytime (the birds are most active in the morning—fed at 9:30 A.M.). You can also watch sea lions through an underwater viewing window. Throughout the day, "Keeper Encounters" take place during animal feeding sessions. A souvenir shop and a restaurant overlook the park. The zoo is connected to MOTAT by an electric tram that runs every 20 minutes along the one-km (0.6-mi) route.

Waitakere Ranges Regional Parkland

This spectacular chunk of wilderness lies on the north side of Manukau Harbour, west of Auckland (continue west along Hwy. 16 from Western Springs, then take Hwy. 19 through Titirangi). It encompasses much of the Waitakere Ranges. Formed by volcanic action about 17 million years ago, the Waitakere Ranges comprise a steep eastern face, rugged valleys, rivers, streams, and waterfalls, which cascade dramatically to the Tasman Sea. A network of nearly 150 "walks" (suitable for everyone) and "tracks" (for the more experienced hiker) covers a distance of more than 200 km (124 mi) (many trails are impassable after high rainfall). The main road through the park traverses the main range and ends at **Piha,** a small seaside community at the protected south end of a beach continuously lashed by massive waves. North and south of Piha, the coastline is no less rugged, with trails leading to secluded beaches and rocky cliffs.

Start a park visit at **Arataki Visitor Centre** (09/366-2000; Sept.–Apr. daily 9 A.M.–5 P.M., May–Aug. Mon.–Fri. 10 A.M.–4 P.M. and Sat.–Sun. 9 A.M.–5 P.M.), five km (3.11 mi) beyond Titirangi. Adorned by Maori carvings, this grand building is a lot more than a visitor

center—inside, the whole natural and human history of the Waitakere Ranges is laid out, and paths lead through the surrounding forest and to raised lookout platforms. Before continuing farther into the park, pick up the excellent *Recreation and Track Guide*—it gives a good overview of the various walks.

SOUTH OF DOWNTOWN
Mount Eden

Head to the top of this extinct volcano, the highest point in Auckland at 196 meters (640 ft), for a 360-degree view of the city. Walking tracks lead around and into the large egg-shaped depression at the top where the crater used to be. It was used as an ancient Maori fortress by the Waiohua people, and their storage pits and defense terraces remain around the outside. The inner crater area shows no signs of occupation, as it was considered sacred to Matuaho, God of Volcanoes. On the lower slopes of the hill lies **Eden Garden** (daily 9 A.M.–4:40 P.M.; free), a colorful array of camellias, azaleas, and rhododendrons planted in the early 1970s. From downtown you can walk to Mount Eden in about 1.5 hours (follow the Coast to Coast Walkway signs), or catch a bus from the downtown bus terminal for Mount Eden and Khyber Pass Roads. Mountain Road takes you to the summit. You can also drive to the top.

◖ One Tree Hill

Situated among the 60-odd volcanic cones dominating Auckland's skyline, One Tree Hill is another prominent dormant volcano (182 meters/600 ft) offering spectacular views over Auckland. It's thought to have last erupted 20,000 years ago, and in the preceding years and before European colonization up to 5,000 Maori lived on its slopes. To the Maori, it was known as Te Totara-i-ahua after the solitary *totara* tree planted on the summit in 1640. The name survived, although the original tree was cut down in the 1850s and

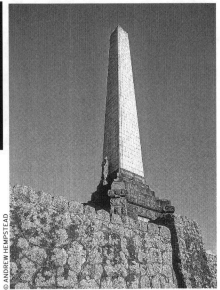

© ANDREW HEMPSTEAD

A monument at the top of One Tree Hill is dedicated to Maori-European friendship.

a replacement Monterey pine succumbed to a combination of vandalism and disease in the 1990s. Surrounding the hill is **Cornwall Park,** farmland deeded to the city by John Logan Campbell in 1900. Today, sheep and cattle still graze on the grassed terraces, and you can rest in the shade of an olive grove planted by Campbell. From Greenlane West (take the Hwy. 9 exit from Hwy. 1), a road winds through the park and around the hill,

eventually reaching the summit as a narrow paved thoroughfare barely wide enough for one vehicle. At the top is an obelisk.

On the southern slopes of One Tree Hill (near the Manukau Road entrance) is **Stardome Observatory** (09/624-1246; adult $12, senior $10, child $6). Displays in the foyer area are open Monday 10 A.M.–3 P.M. and Tuesday–Friday 9:30 A.M.–4:30 P.M., but the real reason to visit is the multimedia presentation showcasing our solar system and beyond, which includes images of the night sky displayed on a large screen via a "sky projector." It plays Tuesday–Sunday at 8 P.M. and is followed at 9 P.M. by a space-oriented documentary. After the show, weather permitting, view the Southern Cross and other Southern Hemisphere stars from the observatory (included in the ticket price).

Auckland Botanic Gardens

This extensive 65-hectare garden lies 27 km (17 mi) south of downtown beside Highway 1. As far as botanic gardens go, they are fairly recent, having been initially developed in 1973 and opened in 1982. The former farm has been transformed, now boasting more than 10,000 plants from around the world. Within the garden is a visitor center (09/266-7158; Mon.–Fri. 8 A.M.–4:30 P.M., Sat.–Sun. 9 A.M.–5 P.M.), a small library, and a café (09/269-3409; daily 8 A.M.–4 P.M.; $11–16) serving light snacks during lunch hours. Admission is free.

Recreation

HARBOR CRUISES

There are so many ways to cruise Waitemata Harbour that your first stop should be the attractively renovated Ferry Building on Quay Street. You'll find **Fullers** (09/367-9111, www.fullers.co.nz) on the ground floor. Fullers runs scheduled transportation and tours to all the populated islands of Hauraki Gulf, as well as to Devonport on the North Shore and around the harbor itself. One of the best ways to enjoy the harbor is to join the 90-minute **Harbour Cruise** (departs daily 10:30 A.M. and 1:30 P.M.; adult $38, senior $35, child $18).

To Devonport

While the Harbour Cruise stops only briefly at Devonport, there's so much to do in and around this North Shore suburb that it's easy to spend a day exploring the area. It's a picturesque place—from the sandy beach beside the ferry terminal, the main street leads uphill past outdoor cafés, art galleries, and trendy boutiques. From the waterfront, a one-km/0.62-mi (20-minute) walking path leads along the harbor east to **North Head,** a historic reserve once an important base for army operations toward the end of the 19th century. Walking tracks lead to many underground tunnels and chambers, gun emplacements and batteries, and a good viewing point. Nearby **Mount Victoria,** an extinct volcanic cone rising 85 meters (280 ft), offers panoramic views of the harbor; a walking track leads to the top.

The least expensive way to cross the harbor is aboard the **Devonport Ferry,** operated by Fullers (09/367-9111; adult $9 round-trip, senior $11, child $5.80; free with a Harbour Cruise ticket) from the Ferry Building. Departures are every 30 minutes 6:15 A.M.–8 P.M., then hourly (on the hour) until 10 P.M.

◖ Sailing

Pride of Auckland (09/373-4557, www.prideofauckland.com) operates a fleet of 45-foot charter yachts, easily recognized by their distinctive blue-and-white sails, from beside the maritime museum. Options include a 50-minute Sailing Experience ($48), a 90-minute lunchtime trip departing daily at 1 P.M. ($70), a 90-minute Coffee Cruise departing at 3 P.M. ($60), and a 2.5-hour dinner trip departing at 7 P.M. that includes a healthy seafood meal cooked on board ($95).

Or you can get *really* serious and step aboard yachts that competed for the America's Cup. A two-hour sailing trip costs adult $160, child $115, or you can pay adult $210, child $180 to participate in a three-hour race-like setting with the two yachts racing against each other. For information, contact **Sail NZ** (Viaduct Harbour, 09/359-5987 or 0800/724-569, www.explorenz.co.nz).

WALKING TRACKS

The local council has done an admirable job of creating an extensive network of walking paths within city limits. The information center stocks related brochures, or head down to the experts at the **Department of Conservation** office in the Ferry Building (137 Quay St., 09/379-6476; Mon.–Fri. 9:30 A.M.–5 P.M., Sat. 10 A.M.–3 P.M.). The **Auckland Council** website (www.aucklandcouncil.govt.nz) is another good source of walking trail information.

Coast to Coast Walkway

This well-marked urban walkway crosses the 16 km (10 mi) of land that separate the Pacific Ocean on the east from the Tasman Sea on the west. Take in tremendous views of the city and the main harbors; climb five volcanic peaks; saunter through parks, gardens, and woods; and listen to native birds on this remarkable track. It's a great way to appreciate the old and the new, the land and the water that make up

Auckland today. The walk starts from downtown's Princes Wharf, and at an easy pace takes about four hours to cover the 13-km (8-mi) trail through the Domain, Mount Eden, and One Tree Hill to suburban Onehunga on Manukau Harbour. A pamphlet containing a detailed map of the route, distances and average walking times, places of interest, viewing points, and parks and gardens is available from the Department of Conservation office.

Point to Point Walkway

It takes about three leisurely hours to do this 7.5-km (4.6-mi) well-marked walk, which starts on Tamaki Drive above St. Heliers Bay and meanders through parks, paddocks, and two nature reserves before ending at Point England. Catch tremendous views of the city from St. John's Ridge before finishing on St. John's Road. If you want to walk around the **Tahuna-Torea Nature Reserve** (Gathering Place of the Oyster-Catcher) along the way, add about 1.5 hours, including time-outs for bird-watching.

BEACHES
Close to Town

Beaches lie on all sides of Auckland, some surprisingly close to the city center, ranging from sheltered sandy coves on the east to pounding surf and black sand on the west. Tamaki Drive leads south out of downtown along the waterfront toward Mission Bay, Kohimaramara Beach, and St. Heliers Bay. The many sheltered beaches along the Tamaki waterfront are popular, offering good, safe swimming and calm water. The first, **Judges Bay,** is only minutes from the city center, accessible from Parnell Rose Gardens. Farther along is **Mission Bay,** known for an attractive fountain that dances at the push of a button. Here you can rent bicycles, catamarans, and windsurfers (sailboards); in summer it's usually packed. Beyond **St. Heliers Beach** is access to **Lady's** (men and women welcome) and **Gentleman's Bays**

(men only), Auckland's two nude beaches. All along Tamaki Drive are boat anchorages, boat launches, changing rooms, and cafés; buses leave from the downtown bus terminal.

North Shore

Over Auckland Harbour Bridge to the North Shore are many more beaches to choose from. **Takapuna Beach** is one of the best known and probably most crowded, but nine others are accessible by bus from Devonport, linked to downtown by ferry.

Along the West Coast

On the west coast lie kilometers of wind- and surf-swept beaches, many quite isolated. They're beautiful but can also be dangerous; they are known for large, unpredictable swells and strong riptides. It's safest to swim at the beaches where the local surf lifesaving club is patrolling. **Piha** is a popular surf beach, patrolled in summer, as are North Piha, Karekare, and Te Henga, all within Waitakere Ranges Regional Parkland. South of Piha, the west coast meets Manukau Harbour along the sandy shores of desolate **Whatipu Beach** (accessible along Huia Rd. from Titirangi), with large sand dunes and good surfing and bird-watching.

In addition to its large surf, **Muriwai Beach,** 45 km (28 mi) from Auckland along Highway 16, is known for a long black-sand (rutile) beach, extensive sand dunes, a gannet colony, and a seaside golf course. A track leads south from the beach to **Maori Bay,** where you'll see unusual geological formations known as "pillow lavas." Behind the beach lies the small community of Muriwai, with a motor camp and fish-and-chips shop.

CYCLING

For information on cycling around the city, contact the **Auckland Cycle Touring Association** (www.acta.org.nz), which organizes rides most weekends. A popular bike route around Auckland covers about 50 km (31 mi) and takes at least three hours. If you ride at a leisurely pace over a full day you'll have the opportunity to visit many city attractions along the route. A map is available from the Auckland Visitor Centre (corner of Victoria and Federal Sts., 09/363-7182; daily 8 A.M.–8 P.M.).

Many bicycle shops rent bikes, including **Adventure Cycles** (9 Premier Ave., Western Springs, 09/940-2453; Thurs.–Mon. 7:30 A.M.–7 P.M.), which rents by the day or week. For those planning an extended cycling trip, rental rates are very reasonable ($100–150 per week), with panniers ($40 per week) also rented. Rentals are also available at many public places around town: Mission Bay, Okahu Bay, the waterfront, and Devonport on the North Shore. Expect to pay about $40–50 per day.

Entertainment and Events

Current information and show times for music, opera, cabarets, theater, dance, and exhibitions are listed in weekend editions of local newspapers. For musical events, the *NZ Herald* gives thorough coverage of what and where, and the Auckland Visitor Centre also has lots of information on Auckland entertainment.

Major cultural and sporting events can be booked through **Ticketek** (Level 2, Aotea Centre, Queen St., 09/307-5060, www.ticketek.co.nz).

SKYCITY

This large entertainment complex (corner of Victoria and Federal Sts. at the base of the Sky Tower, 09/363-6000) holds a wide variety of eateries and lounges, two casinos, and one of Auckland's most luxurious accommodations. The main casino room holds 100 gaming tables (blackjack, stud poker, roulette, Tai Sai, craps, and baccarat) and about 1,500 slot machines. Lounges and bars include avian-themed **Red Hummingbird;** the fine wines of **Twelve Wine Bar; Nations Clubrooms,** a sports bar; **X.O.,** a stylish space with a cocktail menu to match; and **twentyone,** an upscale nightclub, with DJ dance music. **Sky Lounge,** below the main observation level of the Sky Tower, has magnificent views across Hauraki Gulf. **SkyCity Theatre** attracts touring acts and is home to the Auckland Theatre Company. Dinner/theater packages are available to many performances.

THE ARTS

Auckland's main music and performing arts venues are centered around **The Edge** (Queen St., 09/357-3355, www.the-edge.co.nz). On the southern corner of this precinct, the restored Italian Renaissance–style **Auckland Town Hall** comprises two chambers renowned worldwide for their acoustics, the main venues for performances by the **New Zealand Symphony Orchestra** (04/801-3890, www.nzso.co.nz) and **Auckland Philharmonia** (09/638-6266, www.apo.co.nz). Also at The Edge is the 2,380-seat **Civic,** a restored movie palace with an extravagant Eastern-themed art nouveau look, complete with a simulated night sky painted on the ceiling. The Civic hosts touring musicals and shows, occasionally reverting to its original purpose and screening movies. The modern **Aotea Centre** holds two main theater venues. Other organizations performing at these venues include the **Auckland Chamber Orchestra** (09/361-1535; www.aco.co.nz), **Auckland Choral** (09/358-2892, www.aucklandchoral.co.nz), **Chamber Music New Zealand** (04/384-6133, www.chambermusic.co.nz), and **Royal New Zealand Ballet** (04/381-9000, www.nz-ballet.org.nz). For performance details, contact the venue directly; for ticketing information, contact **Ticketek** (Level 2 of the Aotea Centre, 09/307-5060, www.ticketek.co.nz).

On the University of Auckland campus,

Maidment Theatre (8 Alfred St., 09/308-2383) hosts films, concerts, and a large variety of musical and theatrical events throughout the year, including performances produced by the **Auckland Theatre Company** (09/309-0390, www.atc.co.nz).

NIGHTLIFE

In the heart of downtown, a welcoming atmosphere prevails at the historic **Shakespeare Hotel & Brewery** (61 Albert St., 09/373-5396; daily from 11 A.M.), where you can sample a "platter" of traditional beers for $24.

Ensconced in one of the city's most stylish hotels, **Atrium Lounge** (Rendezvous Hotel Auckland, Mayoral Dr., 09/366-5643; Mon.–Sat. from 4:30 P.M.) is a beautifully designed room with a wide-ranging drink list and daily 4:30–5:30 P.M. happy hour.

As always, the hot spots for dancing the night away to DJ music change as regularly as the patrons change their hairstyles. Downtown, the place to be for late-night drinking and dancing is **Margaritas** (18 Elliott St., 09/302-2764), a lounge-style cocktail bar that attracts the over-30 crowd. **Rakinos** (upstairs at 35 High St., 09/358-3535, Thurs.–Sat.) is a quieter place, often with live jazz or reggae. At the top end of Queen Street, Karangahape Road has an inner-city, bohemian feel, with a wide variety of ethnic bars and nightclubs. Upstairs on the busy corner of Queen Street, **Khuja Lounge** (536 Queen St., 09/377-3711) hosts a wide variety of musicians Tuesday–Saturday. Heading west along Karangahape Road from Queen Street, the scene gets sleazy, with strip clubs and sex shops dominating.

In Ponsonby, **Ponsonby Road** has a lively late-night scene, with trendy nightspots and cafés staying open until after midnight. **Lime Bar** (167 Ponsonby Rd., 09/360-7167) and the faux-tropical **Lolabar** (212 Ponsonby Rd., 09/360-0396) are two of the more popular hangouts.

Harborside

The waterfront is an unbeatable location for an afternoon or evening drink. Most of the bars and restaurants along Princes Wharf and around Viaduct Harbour have wonderful outdoor seating areas that take advantage of the bustling waterfront location.

Along the west side of Princes Wharf is a strip of combination bar-restaurants, all perfectly positioned to catch the afternoon sun. Although full menus are offered at all these places, it's generally okay to just order drinks. Although drink prices at **Y-Not** (Shed 23, Princes Wharf, Quay St., 09/359-9998; daily from 10 A.M.) are not as high as elsewhere along the west side of the Princes Wharf, they are even better during happy hour (Mon.–Fri. 4–6 P.M.).

Facing the Ferry Building, **Provedor** (Princes Wharf, Quay St., 09/377-1114; daily from 3 P.M.) has a few palm-fringed tables overlooking the water, but most of the action happens inside this stylish cocktail bar popular with the after-work crowd. Next door, multipurpose **Sanctuary** (Princes Wharf, Quay St., 09/307-1344; daily from 11:30 A.M.) has something for everyone—balcony tables with stunning water views, express weekday lunches that include a drink (from $20), happy hour (weekdays 5–7 P.M.), acoustic performances in an intimate setting (Thurs. from 9:30 P.M.), and one of the city's hippest dance clubs (1st and 3rd Friday of every month).

At the head of Princes Wharf and accessed off the Hilton hotel lobby, **Bellini** (Quay St., 09/978-2025; Mon.–Fri. from 10 A.M., Sat.–Sun. from 9 A.M.) is both one of the city's most stylish bars and its best situated. The crisp, modern decor takes nothing from the stunning water views, but you pay for the privilege—the least expensive drink is a glass of local beer for $8.50, or you can try a namesake champagne and peach cocktail for $21.

At **Freddy's Ice House** (Princes Wharf, Quay St., 09/377-6702; daily from noon), the temperature matches the name. Customers are outfitted with winter clothing before entering a unique bar where everything is frozen, from the walls to the glasses. The cover charge is $27, which includes one cocktail.

Loaded Hog (Viaduct Harbour, 204 Quay St., 09/366-6491), with its own in-house brewery, has huge glass doors that allow everyone to enjoy the sights and sounds of the harbor. While it's a good spot for a quiet drink in the afternoon and evening, a DJ spins disks until 4 A.M. Friday and Saturday. Overlooking the same harbor, **Imperial** (95–99 Customs St. W, 09/377-2720) is a little more pretentious, with a decor to match. **Trench Bar** (Viaduct Harbour, corner Quay and Lower Hobson Sts., 09/309-0412) replicates its namesake—the deepest point of the Pacific Ocean—with dim lighting and sculptures of creatures that inhabit the ocean floor. At the far end of Viaduct Harbour, **O'Hagan's Irish Pub** (101–103 Customs St. W, 09/363-2106) is set back from the water, but offers top-notch food and live Irish outdoor entertainment on Sunday afternoons from 3 P.M.

Backpacker Bars

Globe Bar (229 Queen St. at Darby St., 09/358-4877; daily from 4 P.M.) is part of the Auckland Central Backpackers complex, meaning that it fills nightly with young international travelers looking for cheap drinks and a good time. Also affiliated with backpacker lodges are **First Base** (Base Auckland, 16 Fort St., 09/300-9999) and **Fat Camel** (38 Fort St., 09/307-0181), both with cheap drinks and theme nights throughout the week. The latter hosts a variety of competitions (pool, trivia, etc.) with travel-related prizes for the winners.

FESTIVALS AND EVENTS
Summer

New Zealanders love their sports, so crowds are inevitable when the world's best women tennis players arrive in early January for the **ASB Classic** and the men a week later for the **Heineken Open.** Both tournaments are held at the Auckland

Tennis Centre (1 Tennis Lane, Parnell, 09/373-3623, www.aucklandtennis.co.nz).

Auckland lives up to its "City of Sails" nickname throughout summer, with a variety of events such as match racing; unlike most other yacht races, the emphasis is on the skills of the sailors, who compete in identical yachts in a format that draws huge crowds to the area around Westhaven Marina. Visit the **Royal New Zealand Yacht Squadron** website (www. rnzys.org.nz) for details.

Devonport Food & Wine Festival (www. devonportwinefestival.co.nz) takes place over the second weekend of February in Windsor Reserve on the Devonport waterfront, less than 200 meters (660 ft) from where ferries from downtown dock. Entry is $30, which includes a wine glass used to taste wines from throughout the country at booths set around the treed parkland. Many of Auckland's top restaurants and gourmet food providers are represented and entertainment is provided from two stages.

Fall

Head for Albert Park the first weekend of March for the **Auckland Lantern Festival** (09/379-2020), a colorful celebration of the Chinese New Year that begins at 5 P.M.

Pasifika (09/353-9557) celebrates the culture of the Pacific with traditional island arts, entertainment, sports, and food at Western Springs Park, off Great North Road, on the second weekend of March (Fri. night and all day Sat.). It's most popular with Islanders, but visitors are more than welcome to enjoy the festivities.

The week prior to the Easter break, the country comes to the city as ASB Showground plays host to the **Royal Easter Show** (09/638-9969, www.royaleastershow.co.nz). Expect displays of arts and crafts, livestock and equestrian events, and judging of the national wine awards.

Auckland Art Fair (www.aucklandart-fair.co.nz) fills the Marine Events Centre, at Viaduct Harbour, the middle weekend of May every second (odd) year. Mirroring the wave of similar gatherings around the world, this local version showcases the contemporary work of leading artists from throughout New Zealand.

In late May, literary types congregate at Aotea Centre for the **Auckland Writers and Readers Festival** (www.writersfestival.co.nz). This biennial (odd years) gathering attracts both fiction and nonfiction writers, with a full schedule of public readings and talks.

Winter

The **New Zealand International Film Festival** (www.nzff.co.nz) is a stop for the New Zealand International Film Festivals, which travels around the country showing major films from all over the world. It's held for two weeks through mid-July at venues including the SkyCity Theatre and the Civic. For a schedule and ticketing details, check their website.

Spring

Celebrated on November 5 each year by real kids and grown-up kids, **Guy Fawkes Night** originated in England in 1605. It commemorates the foiling of a conspiracy by Guy Fawkes and his men to blow up London's Parliament buildings and occupants, including King James I, on opening day of Parliament. Nowadays large bonfires, bonfire feasts, spectacular fireworks, and general merriment are the order of the day. Watch the Auckland sky light up; for the best viewing position, head to the top of Mount Eden.

Shopping

In general, shops throughout Auckland are open weekdays 9 A.M.–5 P.M., with some downtown shops, fashionable areas of Parnell and Ponsonby, and most suburban malls also open Saturday 9 A.M.–5 P.M. and Sunday 10 A.M.–3 P.M. Late-night shopping is on Thursday or Friday until 9 P.M.

SHOPPING DISTRICTS

Downtown Queen Street is lined with tourist-oriented and duty-free shops, especially the bottom end. Here you'll also find many currency exchanges. For two floors of shops, specialty stores, coffee lounges, and lunch bars in the city center, visit the Downtown Shopping Centre at Queen Elizabeth Square and Customs Street. In the attractive building that houses the **Old Customhouse Shopping Centre** (22 Customs St. W on the corner of Albert St.) you'll find shops, a restaurant and tavern, and a movie theater. Numerous other shopping arcades with regular shopping hours branch off Queen Street.

Running parallel to Queen Street, High Street and the area around nearby Chancery Street are home to many fashion boutiques, including that of **Karen Walker** (15 O'Connell St., 09/309-6299), one of the country's best-known fashion designers.

Markets are fun to browse at leisure—and they bring out the Aucklanders by droves on weekends, when many other places close. The biggest and most popular market is **Victoria Park Market** (09/309-6911; daily 9 A.M.–6 P.M.), across from Victoria Park and within easy walking distance of downtown. Once Auckland's rubbish destructor and expanded in 2012, its 38-meter (125-ft) chimney can be seen from quite a distance. The cobbled courtyard area swarms with activity as people crowd around colorful vendor carts. The interiors of the former stable buildings have been converted into shops selling art and handcrafts, clothes and jewelry, posters, records, and all sorts of curious knickknacks. On the upper floor you can talk to local artisans and pick up bargains in woven articles, wall hangings, rugs, wool sweaters, pottery, glassware, and leatherwork. The lower floor offers a large variety of ethnic foods in the food hall; food stalls also dot the marketplace. The festive atmosphere is enhanced by daytime entertainment provided by buskers.

Parnell Village is a fun place to browse and buy, but don't forget your travelers checks—it ain't cheap! The village boasts a large variety of specialty shops, boutiques, and courtyard cafés. Cobblestone courtyards; wooden and wrought-iron lacework; steps up and down here, there, and everywhere; and intriguing alleyways leading to equally intriguing shops lure droves of shoppers.

Multicultural **Karangahape Road,** locally referred to as "K Road," is one of Auckland's oldest established shopping areas. You'll find a large variety of cosmopolitan stores and restaurants, a range of shops stocked with Polynesian and Asian foods, and many of the city's theaters in this bustling area.

BOOKSTORES

New Zealanders are prolific readers, and this is reflected in the number of bookstores found throughout the city. Centrally located **Unity Books** (19 High St., 09/307-0731; Mon.–Thurs. 8:30 A.M.–7 P.M., Fri. 8:30 A.M.–8 P.M., Sat.

9 A.M.–6 P.M., Sun. 11 A.M.–6 P.M.) is a friendly independent with a wide selection of New Zealand titles, both fiction and nonfiction. The staff at **Time Out** (432 Mount Eden Rd., Mount Eden, 09/630-3331; daily 9 A.M.–9 P.M.) really know their books, and it shows if you go asking for advice on local literature.

Whitcoulls (210 Queen St. at Victoria St., 09/356-5400; Mon.–Thurs. 8 A.M.–7 P.M., Fri. 8 A.M.–9 P.M., Sat. 9 A.M.–7 P.M., Sun. 10 A.M.–6 P.M.) is the largest bookstore in New Zealand, with multiple floors of books and magazines, and a café. You will find outlets of this chain in most malls and suburbs.

One block east of Queen Street, **Anah Dunsheath Rare Books** (6 High St., 09/379-0379; Tues. and Thurs. 9:30 A.M.–2 P.M.) is an antiquarian bookseller specializing in New Zealand history, the Pacific, and Antarctica. They also carry historical maps and postcards.

OUTLET SHOPS

Perfectly placed for last-minute shopping before reaching the airport is **Dress Smart** (151 Arthur St., 09/622-2400; daily 10 A.M.–5 P.M.), with over 100 outlet shops. In addition to international brands, you can pick up great bargains, including children's clothing from the iconic Pumpkin Patch store.

Accommodations and Camping

Auckland offers a full range of accommodations in all price ranges. As with large cities the world over, major hotel chains have properties in the heart of downtown, but you'll be paying over $200 for a room. Less expensive rooms can be found in the motels that line all highways leading into the city, and you can generally find vacancies at these any time of the year. A unique feature of Auckland's accommodation scene is the large number of backpacker lodges, especially right downtown,

where you can find a bed for the night for less than $25. But be warned: You get what you pay for. The better backpacker lodges can be found in outlying suburbs, such as Parnell. As throughout the country, Auckland has many bed-and-breakfasts. Some favorites are listed below, but a more comprehensive listing can be found in the *New Zealand Bed & Breakfast Book.* Available in bookstores throughout the city, this book will prove invaluable as you travel farther afield.

DOWNTOWN
$50-100

The standard of backpacker lodging in downtown Auckland has improved greatly in the last few years, with established lodges upgrading services to compete with new places.

Surf and Snow (corner Victoria and Albert Sts., 09/363-8889, www.surfandsnow.co.nz, dorm beds $24–35, $58–90 s, $74–100 d) has some of the nicest dorms in downtown, with comfortable mattresses and large lockers.

Halfway up Queen Street from the harbor, **Base Auckland** (229 Queen St., 09/358-4877, www.stayatbase.com, dorm beds $30–34, $80–95 s or d) offers all the usual facilities expected of a large inner-city backpacker lodge—good security, 24-hour Internet access, and lots of room for cooking and relaxing. The lodge has a party bar open to the public and a quieter guest-only lounge. Check the website for discounted rates that include airport transfers and city tours.

YHA New Zealand operates two backpacker lodges in Auckland, both near the top end of Queen Street. **YHA Auckland International** (5 Turner St., 09/302-8200, www.yha.co.nz, dorm beds $25, $66 s, $95–106 d) is a relatively new hostel with its own travel agency, a book exchange, public Internet access, and all the usual facilities such as a communal kitchen, lounge area, TV room, and bike storage. One block up the hill is **YHA Auckland City** (18 Liverpool St., 09/309-2802, www.yha.co.nz, dorm beds $25, $66 s, $95–106 s or d). This renovated hotel has 153 beds in small dormitories and a large number of basic double rooms, as well as a restaurant.

C Jucy Hotel (62 Emily Pl., 09/379-6633, www.jucyhotel.com, $69 s, $72–112 d) is a low-rise accommodation on a quieter downtown street within easy walking distance of the waterfront. The 60 rooms are mostly on the small side. The simple furnishings include LCD TVs in the en suite rooms, while out back is a garden with a barbecue area. As you will note by the distinctive lime-green and purple color scheme, the hotel is affiliated with Jucy Rentals, and all guests receive a discount on car and camper-van rentals, which makes this place an even better value. Rates include underground parking.

The **Shakespeare Hotel & Brewery** (61 Albert St., 09/373-5396, www.shakespearehotel.co.nz, $89–139 s or d) took in its first overnight guests over 100 years ago. Downstairs is a popular bar with great pub food, while upstairs the 10 guest rooms have been given a thorough revamp to offer great value in a very central location one block from SkyCity. All rooms are en suite and some have balconies.

Many city backpacker lodges have nicer rooms than those offered at **Kiwi International Hotel** (411 Queen St., 09/379-6487 or 0800/100-411, www.kiwihotel.co.nz, $79–135 s, $95–135 d), but what this place does have are rooms with en suites and coffeemakers. Other amenities include Internet access, a laundry, a bar, and limited free parking. The hotel is near the top end of Queen Street.

City Lodge (150 Vincent St., 09/379-6183 or 0800/766-686, www.citylodge.co.nz, $75 s, $99–115 d) caters perfectly to travelers simply wanting to rest their head in a comfortable room. Rates are kept low by offering a minimum of services—guest have use of a commercial-style kitchen, relaxing lounge area, and wireless Internet.

$100-200

One of Auckland's original hotels is the **Albion Hotel** (119 Hobson St., 09/379-4900, www.albionhotel.co.nz, $105–150 s or d), dating to 1883. Four blocks west of Queen Street, its rooms are very basic but comfortable with renovated Victorian-style decor, private baths, coffee and tea, fridge, TV, and telephone. Rooms immediately above the street-level bar should be avoided.

A decent choice for budget travelers wanting the privacy of their own room with en suite is

Arena Hotel (131 Beach Rd., 09/303-2463 or 0800/569-888, www.aucklandcityhotel.co.nz, $75 s, $105 d), a few blocks east of downtown but still within walking distance (although cab travel is recommended after dark). The 60 basic rooms have tea- and coffee-making facilities and a small fridge, and local calls are free. Downstairs is a restaurant, bar, Internet terminal, and tour booking desk.

$200–300

A historic downtown department store has been transformed into the **◖ Heritage Auckland** (35 Hobson St., 09/379-8553, www.heritagehotels. co.nz, from $260 s or d), one the city's best-value upscale accommodations (especially if you scoop one of the Web specials, usually advertised for under $200). Public areas in the original wing have retained their 1920s art deco glory, which includes high ceilings and hardwood *jarrah* floors. In addition to well-appointed rooms (many with water views), this property features a fitness room, outdoor and indoor pools, a tennis court, and a casual dining room.

Crowne Plaza Auckland (128 Albert St., 09/302-1111, www.ichotelgroups.com, from $280 s or d) is not as fancy as other properties in this same chain, but since opening in 1991 has gained popularity with business travelers for its services and central location. Many of the rooms have great harbor views and guests enjoy use of a fitness room and the convenience of a restaurant open daily at 6:30 A.M. for breakfast, a lounge, and street-level shopping plaza. Guests on the Executive Club Level ($355 s or d) enjoy upgraded everything, free breakfast, and access to a private lounge. As with all top-end Auckland accommodations, check the hotel website for rooms around $200 *with* breakfast.

CityLife Auckland (171 Queen St., 09/379-9222 or 0800/368-888, www.heritagehotels. co.nz, from $250 s or d) is a spacious business-class hotel with an indoor pool, fitness room, business center, restaurant (daily for breakfast and lunch), and bar. The one-bedroom suites ($290) work well for small families.

Close to the waterfront, the dull exterior of **Copthorne Hotel Auckland** (196 Quay St., 09/377-0349 or 0800/808-228, www.millenniumhotels.com, $280–345 s or d) belies 187 stylish rooms with harbor views and king beds. The street-level restaurant (daily 6:30 A.M.– 10 P.M.) has a good selection of New Zealand cuisine. Online rates are deeply discounted, often to under $150.

Over $300

SkyCity Hotel is part of the impressive SkyCity complex (corner of Victoria and Federal Sts., 09/363-6000 or 0800/759-2487, www.skycity. co.nz). The hotel itself consists of 344 luxurious rooms featuring contemporary furnishings and pleasing nautically inspired pastel color schemes. Other facilities in this full-service hostelry include 24-hour room service, a rooftop heated pool, and a large health club. Within the SkyCity complex itself are 10 eateries and lounges, a casino, and the imposing Sky Tower. Rack rates start at $340 s or d, but check the SkyCity website for packages that include accommodation, breakfast, and Sky Tower tickets for around $240 s or d.

At the waterfront end of Queen Street beside Queen Elizabeth II Square is **Mercure Auckland** (8 Customs St., 09/377-8920, www. mercure.com, $305 s or d), which offers standard rooms with a rack rate higher than it should be, but you should be able to score rooms for under $150 by booking online. Amenities include a fitness room, bar, and restaurant.

Overlooking Viaduct Harbour, **Sebel Suites** (85–89 Customs St., 09/978-4000, www.mirvachotels.com, $335–585 s or d) comprises 129 units with floor-to-ceiling windows, a full kitchen, a laundry facility, and most with a private balcony. Guests also enjoy all the services of a hotel, including room service and underground parking. Although a wide variety of dining options are scattered around Viaduct Harbour, there's no need to look farther than the in-house dining room, Mecca, for top notch food.

With 455 guest rooms, **Rendezvous Hotel Auckland** (Mayoral Dr., 09/366-3000 or 0800/088-888, www.rendezvoushotels.com, $340 s or d) is New Zealand's largest hotel. Each room is spacious and elegantly decorated in earthy tones and has a luxurious granite-lined bathroom. An impressive 12-story-high glass-sided atrium fills the main lobby area with natural light. Other hotel facilities include a fitness room, a business center, and two eateries, including Pacific Restaurant, offering an extensive buffet breakfast. Check the hotel website for rates reduced to under $200 year-round.

The modernistic, crisp white exterior of **C Hilton Auckland** (147 Quay St., 09/978-2000, www.hilton.com, from $448 s or d) is a city landmark. Located at the end of Princes Wharf, it seems to rise from the water, with a design mimicking the sails of boats that fill the surrounding harbor. Public areas and guest rooms are well designed and slick, with sweeping water views from the in-house restaurants and bars as well as from many of the more expensive rooms. Amenities include a heated outdoor lap pool, spa services, valet parking, and room service.

PARNELL

A smattering of privately operated backpacker lodges are along Georges Bay Road, which runs north from Parnell Road, one of the trendiest shopping-and-dining streets in Auckland. Downtown is a 30-minute walk from the choices listed here, and airport shuttle companies will drop you at the front door.

Under $100

The pick of the budget bunch is **City Garden Lodge** (25 St. Georges Bay Rd., 09/302-0880, www.citygardenlodge.co.nz, dorm beds $30-32, $54 s, $70 d). Surrounded by extensive gardens, it's in a grand old building that was once home to the queen of Tonga. The sleeping rooms are clean and bright, with plenty of space to move. The well-manicured garden has a barbecue and plenty of outdoor seating.

The only other backpacker lodge along St. Georges Bay Road worthy of mention, **Lantana Lodge** (60 St. Georges Bay Rd., 09/373-4546, www.lantanalodge.co.nz, dorm beds $27-30, $59 s, $70 d) is also the smallest. It features a well-equipped kitchen, a comfortable TV room and lounge, a porch, friendly management, and plenty of good tourist information on low-budget options. (There's one noisy room, directly below the kitchen—avoid it.)

$100-200

Easily recognized by its stylish blue-and-yellow exterior, the **Parnell Inn** (320 Parnell Rd., 09/358-0642, www.parnellinn.co.nz, $105-140 s or d) is a well-priced motel in the heart of one of Auckland's trendiest suburbs. The 16 fairly

© ANDREW HEMPSTEAD

Hilton Auckland

standard rooms are priced right for the location, with a TV and fridge included; the more expensive rooms have basic cooking facilities. A café is open daily for breakfast, lunch, and dinner.

Parnell City Lodge (2 St. Stephens Ave., 09/377-1463, www.parnellcitylodge.co.nz, $115–150 s or d) features spacious guest rooms, each with a telephone and TV. The more expensive units are very spacious and have kitchens.

Quality Hotel Barrycourt (10 Gladstone Rd., 09/303-3789 or 0800/504-466, www.barrycourt.co.nz, $145–235) is a large motel comprising more than 100 rooms, most with private balconies and large windows that take advantage of filtered harbor views. Standard hotel rooms are $145 s or d, while the larger one- and two-bedroom units, complete with kitchens and distant harbor views, are $175–235.

Over $200

Ascot Parnell (36 St. Stephens Ave., 09/309-9012, www.ascotparnell.com, $185–295 s, $225–395 d) is a charming bed-and-breakfast in a restored 1910 home on a quiet street off busy Parnell Road. It is within walking distance of downtown, and numerous restaurants and cafés are just a short stroll away. The friendly owners make you feel quite at home, and the elegantly furnished rooms are bright, spacious, and paneled in kauri, New Zealand's native timber. Breakfast is a filling affair with almost anything you want, continental or cooked.

WEST OF DOWNTOWN

Ponsonby and Herne Bay are two suburbs immediately west of downtown that hold a number of backpacker lodges—a pleasant alternative to the less personal downtown options. You'll also find bed-and-breakfasts and a couple of solid motel choices.

Under $100

◖ Ponsonby Backpackers (2 Franklin Rd., 09/360-1311, www.ponsonby-backpackers.

co.nz, dorm beds $26–28, $42 s, $56 d) is in a historic two-story house just around the corner from lively Ponsonby Road. The facilities are all of high standards, and the cooking and dining areas are spacious. The staff will store baggage and book tours, and are keen to tell of the latest Ponsonby dining hot spots.

Just off Ponsonby Road, **Red Monkey Traveller's Lodge** (49 Richmond Rd., 09/360-7977, www.theredmonkey.co.nz) is a beautifully restored villa surrounded by lush gardens and a private courtyard lit with lanterns in the evening—soothing music adds to the charm. Inside are excellent communal facilities including an Internet terminal and TV lounge. Most guests book by the week ($240 s, $280 d) in simple single and double rooms with shared facilities, but nightly rates are possible if space is available.

◖ Verandahs (6 Hopetoun St., 09/360-4180, www.verandahs.co.nz, dorm beds $27–31, $55 s, $72 d) is the city's finest backpacker lodge. Backing onto the green space of Western Park, this 1905 kauri-wood villa has been transformed into a home away from home for budget travelers from around the world. Facilities are of the highest standards, including immaculate bathrooms and two kitchens filled with top appliances. Verandahs is just off the top end of Ponsonby Road, a two-minute walk from the free central city bus loop (The Link).

$100-200

Sea Breeze Boutique Motel (213 Jervois Rd., 09/376-2139, www.seabreeze.co.nz, $120–140 s or d) features 10 inviting motel rooms, some with private balconies and harbor views. All rooms have cooking facilities, and a light breakfast is available for $6.

Toward Ponsonby Road from the Sea Breeze, **Abaco on Jervois** (59 Jervois Rd., 09/360-6850 or 0800/220-066, www.abaco.co.nz, $184–274 s or d) is an old motel that has undergone some serious renovations. Each of the 14 rooms has two TVs, a kitchen outfitted with stainless steel appliances, and bathrooms with jetted tubs and in-floor heating.

SOUTH OF DOWNTOWN
$100-200

Bamber Lodge (22 View Rd. off Mount Eden Rd., 09/623-4267, www.hostelbackpacker.com, dorm beds $27, $64–84 s or d) offers 40 beds in a rambling 1910 homestead with spacious grounds and a small pool in a quiet residential area. Everything is spotlessly clean, the rooms are large and bright, the kitchen is fully equipped, and there's a dining area, TV room, and plenty of space for off-street parking.

Another solid choice in Mount Eden is **Oaklands Lodge** (5 Oaklands Rd., 09/638-6545, www.oaklands.co.nz, dorm beds $24, $45 s, $58–68 d), in a quiet residential part of this upmarket suburb. The two-story Victorian-era house features large communal areas and extensive gardens.

A longtime favorite with readers, **◖ Bavaria B&B Hotel** (83 Valley Rd., 09/638-9641, www.bavariabandbhotel.co.nz, $95–110 s, $145–175 d) is a rambling kauri villa dating to the early 1900s. It provides 11 comfortable guest rooms, each with private bath; three rooms also have balconies. In the guest TV lounge you can help yourself to tea or coffee, then enjoy the timber deck that overlooks a subtropical garden. Rates include a buffet-style breakfast and wireless Internet.

NORTH SHORE

Linked to downtown by ferry, the North Shore suburb of Devonport is home to a number of upscale bed-and-breakfasts, or you can choose to stay at a smattering of motels spread through suburbs that extend north to city limits.

$100-200

Near the north end of Auckland Harbour Bridge and backing onto a forested reserve is the **Ocean Inn Motel** (27 Ocean View Rd., Northcote, 09/419-8080 or 0800/820-822, www.oceaninnmotel.co.nz, $110–145 s or d), one of the North Shore's least expensive motels. It features 17 comfortable guest rooms, some with kitchens. Take the Northcote Road exit from the Northern Motorway (Hwy. 1).

Emerald Inn (16 The Promenade, 09/488-3500, www.emerald-inn.co.nz, $175–300 s or d) is five km (3 mi) north of Devonport and 50 meters (0.03 mi) from Takapuna Beach. Each brightly furnished room comes with a fully equipped kitchen and opens to a courtyard filled with greenery and a small outdoor heated pool. Amenities include a laundry, poolside dining room, and barbecue.

Over $200

One of the best Auckland bed-and-breakfasts is the **◖ Peace and Plenty Inn** (6 Flagstaff Terr., 09/445-2925, www.peaceandplenty.co.nz, $195–265 s, $265–465 d), overlooking the water and a one-minute walk from fine restaurants, trendy cafés, intriguing shops, and the ferry terminal. The house was built in 1888 and has been renovated and tastefully decorated. Each of the seven guest rooms features individual character, a comfortable bed, and memorable touches such as fresh flowers and chocolates. The Garden Room, with a private entry and small courtyard surrounded by a scented garden, is a particular delight. In the lounge, guests can browse through the well-stocked library while enjoying complimentary tea, coffee, or port. Breakfast, in a dining area overlooking a tropical garden, is a memorable event featuring a delicious choice of fresh fruits and hot dishes such as Belgian waffles prepared by host Judy Machin.

Along with having a number of upscale bed-and-breakfasts, the harborside suburb of Devonport is home to the grand old **Esplanade Hotel** (1 Victoria Rd., 09/445-1291, www.esplanadehotel.co.nz, from $290 s or d), built in 1903 and last renovated in 2002. It stands opposite the ferry terminal, separated only by landscaped gardens, and at the end of a street chock-full of cafés and restaurants—the perfect city escape. The owners have refurnished 17 guest rooms with simple yet stylish pieces, including cane furniture.

MANGERE (AIRPORT)

The following accommodations are within an eight-km (five-mi) radius of the airport, and each provides airport transfers.

Airport Skyway Lodge (30 Kirkbride Rd., 09/275-4443, www.skywaylodge.co.nz, dorm beds $25, $59–89 s or d) offers a swimming pool and a communal kitchen (it's also within walking distance of a couple of restaurants). The most basic rooms share bathrooms, or you can stay in an en suite room.

Nearby, the 37-room **Auckland Airport Inn** (190 Kirkbride Rd., 09/275-5082, www.auck-landairportinn.co.nz, $90–140 s or d) offers extensive landscaping around a swimming pool, complete with barbecue facility and playground. It's a five-minute drive from the airport.

The faux-Tudor **Oakwood Manor Motor Lodge** (610 Massey Rd., 09/275-0539 or 0800/801-555, www.silveroaks.co.nz, $145–195 s or d) is a large complex that surrounds an open courtyard. It has an outdoor pool and a small restaurant.

HOLIDAY PARKS
South of Downtown

The closest camping to downtown Auckland is at **Remuera Motor Lodge,** four km (2.5 mi) southeast of the city center (16 Minto Rd. off Remuera Rd., Remuera, 09/524-5126, www.remueramotorlodge.co.nz, campsites $20–28 per person). It is surrounded by trees and has a large swimming pool and landscaped camping area. There are relatively few flat grassy spots for tents, but there is a lot of space for RVs.

Avondale Motor Park (46 Bollard Ave., Avondale, 09/828-7228 or 0800/100-542, www.aucklandmotorpark.co.nz, tent sites $18 per person, powered sites $25 s, $40 d, cabins and flats $60–90 s or d) is nine km (5.5 mi) southwest of the city off New North Road, close to MOTAT and the zoo. Amenities are limited, but the more expensive tourist flats are an excellent value.

North Shore

North Shore Motels and Holiday Park (52 Northcote Rd., Takapuna, 09/418-2578 or 0508/909-090, www.nsmotels.co.nz, campsites $30 s, $40 d, dorm beds $48, basic cabins $68, en suite motel rooms $145 s or d). There are plenty of grassy sites, with facilities catering to campers, motor-home travelers, or those who prefer their own private cabin. All guests have the use of an indoor swimming pool, TV lounge, large communal bathroom, kitchen blocks, and laundry. To get there from the city center, cross the Harbour Bridge in the Whangarei lane. Four km (2.5 mi) north, take the Northcote Road exit (not the Northcote-Birkenhead exit) and turn left. In less than one km (0.6 mi), look for the sign and take the driveway on the far side of the Pizza Hut restaurant.

Also in Takapuna is **Takapuna Beach Holiday Park** (22 The Promenade, 09/489-7909, www.takapunabeachholidaypark.co.nz, campsites $42–47, cabins $65–95 s or d, motel rooms $125). As the name suggests, it's right on the beach, and some powered sites have a fantastic waterfront location. Amenities include a laundry, barbecue, and public Internet access.

Food

The food scene in Auckland has improved almost beyond recognition in the last two decades. From meat pies now filled with gourmet delicacies to a coffee culture as serious as seen anywhere in the world and waterfront restaurants keeping up with the latest trends, the changes have infiltrated all levels of price and style. As in North America, eating healthy has become more important, so you will find many of the better restaurants incorporating this philosophy with local produce and game, which naturally includes an abundance of seafood.

Auckland has no distinct "dining precinct," but the west side of downtown's **Princes Wharf** and adjacent **Viaduct Harbour** have the main concentrations of upscale dining, with outdoor dining and water views as a bonus.

A concentration of upscale restaurants can be found along the western side of Princes Wharf.

DOWNTOWN
Cafés

Cafés line most downtown streets. As is the case throughout New Zealand, you will be impressed by the quality and presentation of freshly brewed coffee, which is nearly always espresso and only very rarely filter-style. High Street, one block east of Queen Street, is popular with urbanites for its profusion of happening cafés. Coffee hot spots include **Columbus Coffee** (Metropolis Building, 43 High St., 09/309-5677), with coffees from around the world, and **Paneton Cafe** (60 High St., 09/303-2515). Both open weekdays at 7 A.M. and weekends at 9 A.M.

Vulcan Lane, linking High Street to the much busier Queen Street, is home to a personal favorite for breakfast—◖ **Café Melba** (33 Vulcan Lane, 09/300-7340; Mon.–Fri. 7 A.M.–4 P.M., Sat.–Sun. 8 A.M.–4 P.M.), where service is friendly yet professional. Breakfast and lunch dishes include offerings such as salmon hash ($12.50), comprising poached eggs and hollandaise sauce on a bed of smoked salmon and mashed potato.

The grandly named **Mecca** (Chancery Square, Chancery St., 09/356-7028; Mon.–Fri. 7 A.M.–10:30 P.M., Sat. 8 A.M.–10:30 P.M., Sun. 8 A.M.–6 P.M.), just off High Street, has more tables outside than inside and a grand central outdoor serving area covered by a high circular roof. As one of the first Auckland cafés with Wi-Fi access and as part of a local chain renowned for top-notch coffee, this place hums day and night. With dishes such as mixed-berry-and-ricotta hotcakes and pan-fried snapper doused in hollandaise sauce, you are encouraged to stay for more than just a drink.

In the vicinity of Mecca, **Pavilion** (48 Shortland St., 09/359-9466; Mon.–Sat. from 7 A.M.) overlooks a courtyard from beside the lobby of the Royal & Sun Alliance Building.

It fills with workers from the law and insurance firms above, but don't let this put you off. A popular breakfast dish is corn fritters with bacon, avocado, tomato, and chutney ($14.50).

Many of the restaurants on Princes Wharf and around Viaduct Harbour welcome visitors to stop by for coffee and a light meal, allowing you to enjoy a waterfront setting without the high price of a full meal; **Barabra** (Princes Wharf, 09/966-0444; daily from 8 A.M.) is one of the best choices for a coffee. Easily missed in this part of the city is the **Waterfront Café** (14 Quay St., 09/359-9914; daily 9 A.M.–9 P.M.), beside the maritime museum complex. Tiered seating means everyone has a view of the historic vessels out front, but the prime tables lie over the water. Expect to pay $12–28 for dishes as varied as salmon panini and lamb shanks with garlic mash.

Chinese

Yum cha (also called dim sum in New Zealand, although there is a difference), the Chinese lunchtime tradition that allows you to choose items from a trolley as it's wheeled past your table, is popular throughout Auckland. Expect bamboo baskets of steaming goodies such as dumplings, won ton, and spring rolls, as well as a huge array of sickly sweet and savory desserts.

At **Ding How Chinese Restaurant** (55 Albert St., 09/358-4838; Mon.–Fri. 11:30 A.M.–2:30 P.M., Sat.–Sun. 9:30 A.M.–2:30 P.M., and daily from 5:30 P.M.; $16–30), *yum cha* is a traditional affair and is always busy with Asian families. Dinner mains are mostly under $25, although you'll pay more for classic Peking duck, for which Ding How is best known.

Not much English is spoken at the **Mandarin Seafood Restaurant** (47 Hobson St., 09/377-2886; Mon.–Sat. lunch and dinner; $12–16), but *yum cha* is ridiculously inexpensive—and besides, not knowing what you're getting is half the fun.

Contemporary

At **Euro Bar** (west side of Princes Wharf, Quay St., 09/309-9866; daily noon–midnight; $28–45), beautiful Aucklanders gather to see and be seen, with a lucky few snatching an outdoor table to catch the last rays of evening sun as it sets over the harbor. The chef is noted for his use of organic produce and local game in dishes such as baked duck breast with spiced pear truffle and shallot puree.

Most of the restaurants along the western side of Princes Wharf are adult oriented, and so is **[Y-Not** (Princes Wharf, Quay St., 09/359-9998; Mon.–Fri. from 10 A.M., Sat.–Sun. from 10 A.M. for lunch and dinner; $28–36), which seamlessly blends hip decor with a welcoming ambience. But Y-Not also has a menu especially for children, leaving the grown-ups to dine on a mouthwatering lunchtime seafood salad or roast ostrich on a bed of steamed bok choy for dinner.

On the ground floor of the perfectly placed Ferry Building, **Cin Cin on Quay** (99 Quay St., 09/307-6966; daily 10 A.M.–10 P.M.; $32–42) has great water views and a classical feel, with high arched doorways and elegant table settings both inside and out. Start with freshly shucked oysters (from $4.50 each), then tuck into the likes of lamb cutlets infused with Asian spices or a rich bouillabaisse filled with local seafood.

Most major downtown hotels have dining rooms. One of the best of these is **Pacific Restaurant** (Rendezvous Hotel Auckland, Mayoral Dr., 09/366-3000; daily for breakfast and dinner; $28–35), a stylish space off the main lobby. The continental buffet breakfast is $22 and the cooked version is $30. In the evening, mains such as steamed game fish with bean and corn salsa are under $35.

European

Classic European cuisine is overshadowed in Auckland by restaurants adding a local twist to region-specific cooking in a modern setting. **Limon** (Princes Wharf, Quay St., 09/358-5402; Mon.–Fri. from 11 A.M., Sat.–Sun. from 10 P.M.; $26–32) is a perfect example. One of the hip eateries along the west side of Princes Wharf, its menu is decidedly Mediterranean, with mains such as calamari in tomato sauce and grilled lamb skewers with hummus and tzatziki; the rhubarb and ginger pudding is a delicious way to end your meal.

In an attempt to re-create the small, back-alley restaurants you may find in Madrid, **Tasca** (Vulcan Lane, 09/309-6300; Mon.–Fri. 7:30 A.M.–10 P.M., Sat.–Sun. 8:30 A.M.–10 P.M.; $18–29) is a little more traditional than Limon. The tapas menu allows you to choose as much or as little as you like to eat (I loved the *cordero*—lamb roasted in pomegranate molasses).

Serious foodies will appreciate the **❮ French Café** (210 Symonds St., 09/377-1911; Fri. for lunch, Tues.–Sat. for dinner; $32–43) for its perfectly presented, flavor-filled contemporary European cuisine. The French Café is consistently regarded as one of the city's best restaurants, and the food is accompanied by professional service and original artwork on sparkling white walls.

Market

Victoria Park Market (210–218 Victoria St., 09/309-6911; daily 9 A.M.–6 P.M.), west of downtown on Victoria Street, has food stalls scattered throughout. They sell a wide range of Western and ethnic food: everything from pies and hot dogs to falafels, pasta dishes, and Chinese meals. If you're lucky, a band will be playing in the outdoor eating area, and even if it rains, you can still enjoy the food and free jazz by seeking shelter under the large table umbrellas.

Mexican and South American

The **Mexican Café** (67 Victoria St., 09/373-2311; daily noon–10 P.M.; $21–25) is colorfully decorated with traditional Mexican motifs and has a small outdoor patio. The food is good and inexpensive, with all mains under $25.

Some of Auckland's freshest and most flavorful Mexican food is prepared at **Mexicali**

Fresh (Princes Wharf, 137 Quay St., 09/307-2419; Sun.–Thurs. 11 A.M.–9 P.M., Fri.–Sat. 11 A.M.–10 P.M.; $15–22.50), on the east side of Princes Wharf. Each dish is made from scratch, yet the prices don't reflect the extra attention and care. Delicious margaritas and Mexican coffee add to the appeal.

Wildfire (Princes Wharf, Quay St., 09/353-7595; daily noon–midnight) is a Brazilian *churrasco*, or barbecue restaurant, featuring favorite dishes from the south of the country. Pay $40 per person before 7 P.M. or $55–75 after for unlimited food, including beef, pork, chicken, and lamb, carved at the table from long skewers of meat that has been marinated then slowly char-grilled over hot coals.

Seafood

Seafood is a feature throughout Auckland, including at many of the restaurants serving contemporary cuisine.

To truly immerse yourself in the local seafood culture, plan on rising early to attend the 6 A.M. auction at the **Auckland Fish Market** (22–32 Jellicoe St., 09/379-1490). The market remains open daily until 7 P.M. with a number of excellent dining choices. My favorite market dining experience is **Oceanz** (09/303-3416; Mon.–Fri. 10 A.M.–6 P.M., Sat.–Sun. 9 A.M.–6:30 P.M.; $12–16), which cooks up the freshest fish and chips imaginable. Order them to go and wander down to enjoy them at Viaduct Harbour for the full effect.

Upstairs in the Ferry Building at **Harbourside** (99 Quay St., 09/307-0486; daily 11:30 A.M.–10:30 P.M.; $31–45), seafood is the specialty. The menu takes its inspiration from around the world, but local seafood dominates, with dishes like clam and mussel chowder to start and mains such as grilled game fish marinated in soy, ginger, and lime. Crayfish, plucked live from a huge tank, are also popular and can be steamed, grilled, or roasted—the choice is yours. New Zealand vino dominates the long wine list.

© ANDREW HEMPSTEAD

For the city's freshest seafood, head to the Auckland Fish Market.

Kermadec (Viaduct Harbour, corner of Quay and Lower Hobson Sts., 09/309-0412; daily for lunch and dinner; $29–42) stands out for its striking nautical-theme decor throughout five dining areas. For a casual meal, it's difficult to top the brasserie and starters such as king prawns and squid with papaya and honey chili dressing. Then, for the main course, simply choose a fish type and decide whether you'd like it steamed, char-grilled, or deep-fried.

Thai

You'll find inexpensive westernized Thai restaurants scattered throughout downtown and the suburbs. One of the better choices is **Mai Thai Restaurant** (corner of Victoria and Albert Sts., 09/366-6258; Mon.–Fri. noon–3 P.M., Mon.–Sat. 6–10:30 P.M.; $15–24), upstairs in the yellow building between Queen Street and SkyCity. The set lunch is $18, while the dinner menu features pad Thai for $15 and duck, prawns, and shrimp dishes all under $25.

Moving up in style, there are a few upscale places that offer more traditional Thai cooking at reasonable prices relative to other top city restaurants. One of these is **Khao** (corner Chancery and O'Connell Sts., 09/377-5088; Mon.–Fri. noon–2:30 P.M. and 5:30–10:30 P.M., Sat. 5:30–10:30 P.M.; $19–29), at street level of the imposing Chancery Towers, a Gothic Revival building dating to 1925. The restaurant itself is anything but historic, with a stylish open-plan setting. Prawn cakes make a delicious starter, and you can stick with the seafood theme by ordering whole snapper. The curries are also good.

SKYCITY

This massive complex on the corner of Victoria and Federal Streets (09/363-6000) features a number of eateries. The first one you'll spy is **Rebo** (daily 7 A.M.–11 P.M.; $15–29), a stylish street-level café serving up bistro-style fare such as gourmet pizza. The buffet spread

LOCAL SEAFOOD

Snapper, hake, orange roughy, *hapuka* (grouper), kingfish, tuna, and swordfish are all caught along the North Island's east coast. Oysters, mussels, crayfish, crabs, and prawns are also available. The best place to enjoy this abundance of fresh seafood in Auckland is at one of the many restaurants along the harbor. Not only do these eateries have wonderful locations for enjoying the sights, sounds, and smells of the ocean, much of the seafood comes straight from the fishing boats to the table. In the case of **Kermadec,** the fishing company owns the restaurant.

In this same part of the city are several fish markets, busiest before dawn, when the trawlers have docked and local restaurateurs are searching out their favorite catch. At the **Auckland Fish Market** (22-32 Jellicoe St., 09/379-1490; daily 6 A.M.-7 P.M.), about 20 tons of seafood are sold by auction each morning beginning at 6 A.M. Although there's a public viewing gallery, there are plenty of reasons to return later in the day, when you'll find outlets selling everything from live crabs to eel, a take-out sushi bar, a fish-and-chips stand, a café, and a cooking school.

© ANDREW HEMPSTEAD

The Ferry Building holds two excellent seafood restaurants.

at **Fortuna** is extensive, and the food decent; lunch is $29 (noon–3 P.M.) and dinner is $45 (5:30–10:30 P.M.). Kids pay half the adult price. Overlooking the foyer of SkyCity is **Ming Court,** a small Chinese restaurant open daily for dim sum lunch ($18 all-you-can-eat) and à la carte dinner.

Named for the New Zealand–born celebrity-chef owner, **dine by Peter Gordon** (daily 5:30–10:30 P.M.; $36–51) is a classically elegant room with perfectly presented fusion food that uses the very best local ingredients.

Immediately above the main observation decks of the Sky Tower is **Orbit** (daily 11:30 A.M.–2:30 P.M. and 5:30–9:45 P.M.; $31–45), an upscale revolving restaurant with creative dishes such as prawn and capsicum fritters and maple-and-soy-marinated venison. Above Orbit is the **Observatory,** a buffet restaurant open Friday to Sunday for lunch (11:30 A.M.–2 P.M.; adult $49, child $35) and daily for dinner (6–9 P.M.; adult $69, child $45). Prices include access to the Sky Tower.

PARNELL

You'll find many of Aucklanders' favorite restaurants in the Parnell area. Named for a group of 1960s psychedelic rockers, **Strawberry Alarm Clock** (119 Parnell Rd., 09/377-6959; Mon.–Fri. 7 A.M.–5 P.M., Sat.–Sun. 8:30 A.M.–4:30 P.M.; $8–16) attracts an eclectic crowd ranging from students to local business owners. Exposed brick walls, a painted concrete floor, and worn timber furniture all add to the funky atmosphere. The menu features lots of healthy fare, as well as hot breakfasts and some deliciously innovative salads.

Farther up the hill, **Verve** (311 Parnell Rd., 09/379-2860; Mon.–Fri. 7:30 A.M.–5 P.M., Sat.–Sun. 8 A.M.–5 P.M.; $8–15) offers a generous breakfast, as well as attractive sandwiches and interesting salads at prices that are surprisingly attractive for Parnell.

Continuing up the hill, **Non Solo Pizza** (259 Parnell Rd., 09/379-5358; daily noon–midnight; $18–30) offers gourmet pizzas, but as the name suggests, "not only pizza," with choices as varied as a modern take on moussaka and steaming bowls of pasta for up to four diners to share (from $16 per person).

Athidi on Parnell (323 Parnell Rd., 09/358-2969; Tues.–Sun. from 5:30 P.M.; $19–31) features contemporary East Indian cuisine in a smart setting (terrace seating is a delight). The menu isn't large, but it features classics like butter prawns in *masala* served with basmati rice ($31). Vegetarian delicacies include *Navrattan Korma* (mixed vegetables stir-fried in a cashew-and-almond-flavored gravy).

Just south of Parnell, in Newmarket, **Bodrum Cafe** (2 Osborne St., 09/529-1931; Tues.–Sun. from 6 P.M.; $15–25) has a wide selection of Turkish and Middle Eastern dishes starting at $15, including char-grilled spicy lamb kebabs.

PONSONBY

Don't let a local calling this neighborhood "Ponsnobby" put you off experiencing the dining delights of this historic suburb just west of downtown. Ponsonby Road holds dozens of hip cafés and restaurants, many of which stay open until midnight—but I'll start with breakfast. **◖ The Food Room** (250 Ponsonby Rd., 09/360-2425; Mon.–Fri. 7:30 A.M.–5 P.M., Sat. 8 A.M.–4:30 P.M., Sun. 9 A.M.–4:30 P.M., $8) has some of the best pies in the city, including chicken and creamy mushroom, egg and bacon, and steak and kidney.

Escape the crowds of Ponsonby Road to **Coffee Supreme** (42 Douglas St., 09/360-5040; Mon.–Fri. 7 A.M.–3 P.M., Sat. 8 A.M.–3 P.M.), where you'll find some of the city's best coffee, sourced from around the world and roasted in-house daily. **Blake St.** (corner of Prosford and Blake Sts., 09/360-6261; Wed.–Sun. 8 A.M.–4 P.M.) also concentrates on pouring gourmet coffee in a relaxed atmosphere.

More than one U.S. reader has written recommending **Burger Wisconsin** (168 Ponsonby Rd., 09/360-1894; daily 11:30 A.M.–10 P.M.; $9–14) for the city's best burgers. Choices include chicken breast with avocado and bacon on a sourdough bun. Another New Zealand burger chain represented in Ponsonby is **Burger Fuel** (114 Ponsonby Rd., 09/378-6466; daily for lunch and dinner; $8–14). Its politically incorrect advertising campaigns get all the attention, but, like Burger Wisconsin, the burgers themselves, far superior to Burger King et al., are the main draw.

Thai cuisine is a popular alternative to Chinese food in New Zealand. One of the better Thai restaurants is **Thai Classic Restaurant** (282 Ponsonby Rd., 09/370-3389; Mon.–Fri. noon–2:30 P.M. and 5:30–10:30 P.M., Sat.–Sun. 5:30–10:30 P.M.; $18–25), a stylish place.

Practicalities

INFORMATION

After passing through immigration and then customs at Auckland International Airport, you'll be ushered down the ramp into the main airport lobby. Head *left* through the crowds to the **Auckland International Airport Visitor Centre** (09/275-6467). It's open seven days a week from 5 A.M. until the day's last flight clears customs and immigration. The information center in the domestic terminal (09/256-8480) is open daily 7 A.M.–5 P.M.

The main downtown information center is the **Auckland Visitor Centre** (corner of Victoria and Federal Sts., 09/363-7182; daily 8 A.M.–8 P.M.) at the street level of SkyCity. By Viaduct Harbour, the **New Zealand Visitor Centre** (137 Quay St., 09/979-7005) is open daily 9:30 A.M.–5:30 P.M.

You'll find a combined **Department of Conservation/Auckland Regional Parks** (09/379-6476; Mon.–Fri. 9:30 A.M.–5 P.M., Sat. 10 A.M.–3 P.M.) information center in the Ferry Building on Quay Street. This center has all the information you need on regional parks, national parks, campgrounds, walks, and the gulf islands. In the same building is the **Fullers Cruise Centre** (09/367-9111, www.fullers.co.nz), the best source of information on travel to the gulf islands.

The **Automobile Association,** or AA, is at 99 Albert Street (09/302-1825; Mon.–Fri. 8 A.M.–4:30 P.M.). Upon proof of any worldwide AA membership, this helpful association provides free maps, information, and general travel advice. Be sure to ask for the current *Accommodation Directory,* invaluable for travel throughout the country.

At **Auckland Central Library** (Lorne St. at Wellesley St., 09/377-0209; Mon.–Thurs. 9:30 A.M.–8 P.M., Fri. until 9 P.M., Sat. 10 A.M.–4 P.M., Sun. 1–5 P.M.), you'll find a

newspaper reading room with current papers from all over New Zealand, as well as some British, Australian, Canadian, and U.S. papers. As in libraries across the country, Internet access is free.

SERVICES

The main post office is in the Bledisloe Building on Wellesley Street. Arriving in Auckland on an international flight, you'll find a currency exchange outlet just beyond customs. Others are located downtown along the lower end of Queen Street. You'll get a slightly better rate at banks, which are generally open weekdays 10 A.M.–4:30 P.M. Most large hotels and stores will cash checks, but the exchange rate leans considerably in their favor (particularly in the tourist shops).

Most downtown hotels and all backpacker lodges have wireless Internet access. **iPlay Internet Café** (33 Lorne St., 09/309-8897) is a centrally located café where Internet access is $5 per hour. It's open 24 hours daily.

For all emergencies, call 111 or **Auckland City Hospital** (Park Rd., 09/379-7440), which has a 24-hour emergency department. For less urgent cases, call **Auckland Metro Doctors** (17 Emily Pl., 09/373-4621; Mon.–Fri. 9 A.M.–5:30 P.M., Sat. 10 A.M.–2 P.M.).

GETTING THERE
By Air

Auckland International Airport (www.aucklandairport.co.nz), New Zealand's largest airport, is 21 km (13 mi) south of downtown. It has separate international and domestic terminals, but they are linked by a free shuttle bus (or by a well-signed walkway). Coming off international flights, and after passing through customs and immigration, the **Visitor Information Centre** (09/275-6467) is off to the left of the reception area. Open for all international flights, it has all the obligatory maps and transportation information. Nearby you'll find a bank of accommodation phones, free Internet access, rental car desks, a gift shop, café, and currency exchange, and phone rentals.

In addition to international flights, the national carrier, **Air New Zealand** (09/336-2400 or 0800/737-300, www.airnewzealand.com), serves cities and towns throughout the country, with Auckland as the main hub.

There are many ways to travel between the airport and downtown. The easiest way is by cab, which costs $50–60 regardless of the number of passengers.

Airbus (09/366-6400 or 0800/105-080, www.airbus.co.nz, adult $28 round-trip) picks up at both terminals and stops at major downtown hotels and backpacker lodges. The service runs every 20 minutes and takes one hour to reach downtown. Door-to-door service is provided by **Super Shuttle** (09/306-3960, www.supershuttle.co.nz), which charges $32 one-way for the first passenger and then $8 for each extra passenger going to the same destination. Book online or call at least one hour in advance.

By Rail

The terminus for long-distance trains is **Britomart Transport Centre** (8–10 Queen St., 09/374-3873, www.britomart.co.nz), across from the harbor at the bottom end of Queen Street. These trains are operated by **KiwiRail** (04/495-0775 or 0800/872-467, www.kiwirail.co.nz), with services south from Auckland to Wellington, Tauranga, and Rotorua.

By Bus

Long-distance bus travel is the most popular form of public transportation for international visitors to New Zealand, and Auckland is the main hub. **Intercity** (www.intercity.co.nz) has services to just about every point of the country. The depot is at the **SkyCity Coach Terminal** (102 Hobson St., 09/583-5780), but for the number of travelers space is limited at

the terminal, with passengers lining the sidewalk during busy periods. The ticket office is open Sunday–Friday 7:15 A.M.–6:15 P.M. and Saturday 7:15 A.M.–2:30 P.M.

GETTING AROUND

Auckland has an excellent transportation network; you can get almost anywhere by bus, train, or ferry. Although the services are provided by private operators, the regional transit system is known as **MAXX** (09/366-6400, www.maxx.co.nz). A Discovery Pass for unlimited bus, train, and ferry transport is $15. **HOP** (www.myhop.co.nz) is a simple payment method for those using public transit.

Britomart Transport Centre

Incorporating Auckland's historic post office, the Britomart Transport Centre (corner of Queen and Quay Sts.) is the terminus for local and long-distance trains and local buses.

Britomart Transport Centre is the hub of downtown transportation.

© ANDREW HEMPSTEAD

It's a large, modern terminal with cafés, a currency exchange, a gift shop, big-screen TVs, and the **Britomart Information Kiosk** (Mon.–Sat. 7:30 A.M.–8 P.M., Sun. 8 A.M.–5 P.M.) all located at street level. Plans for an underground concourse linking the transport center to the ferry terminals, light rail transit, and a subway loop through downtown have been on the drawing board for years, but have yet to come to fruition.

By Bus

Buses cover the entire urban area, with services radiating from the streets surrounding the Britomart Transport Centre on Queen Street at Quay Street, and from suburban hubs in New Lynn and Otahuhu. Buses run Monday–Saturday 6:30 A.M.–11 P.M. and Sunday 6:30 A.M.–7 P.M. Fares begin at $0.50 for travel within the inner city and increase in increments to $10.30 for the maximum distance traveled. **Inner Link** ($1.80) provides an easy way to get around downtown. This efficient service runs every 10–20 minutes daily 6 A.M.–11 P.M. (until midnight on weekends) along Quay Street, up through Parnell to the museum, and back past Aotea Square to Victoria Park Market and Ponsonby.

By Rail

TranzMetro is a commuter rail service that operates as part of **MAXX** (09/366-6400, www.maxx.co.nz). It operates Mon.–Sat. 6 A.M.–8 P.M. The three routes run from the Britomart Transport Centre west to Waitakere via Newmarket, south to Papakura via Newmarket and Penrose, and south to Papakura via Panmure and the eastern suburbs; tickets are $1.40 per stage point.

By Ferry

Fullers (Ferry Building, Quay St., 09/367-9111, www.fullers.co.nz) operates a scheduled service between downtown and Devonport. Ferries depart at least every 30 minutes 6:15 A.M.–7 P.M., then hourly until 11 P.M. daily. The round-trip fare is adult $11, senior $8.60, child $5.40. Fullers also operates scheduled service to Rangitoto, Waiheke, and Great Barrier Islands.

By Car

Auckland has an incredible number of car rental agencies. All the major agencies are represented, but it is the small, lesser-known companies that make up the bulk (more than 80 at last count). As a result of fierce competition, rates are reasonable—it is often possible to get a weekly rate in summer of under $400 from the international companies and under $300 from the local operations.

Major agencies and their local contact numbers include **Avis** (09/379-2650), **Budget** (09/976-2270), **Hertz** (09/367-6350), **National** (09/309-3336), and **Thrifty** (09/309-0111). Each of these agencies has a desk at the airport and outlets throughout downtown.

Scotties (09/303-3912, www.scotties.co.nz), a local agency based in Mount Eden, has a variety of vehicles (and a few campervans) at good prices, and specializes in long-term rentals. The vehicles are newer models and reliable; each is covered by the maximum insurance available. Scotties also has an outlet in Christchurch, the perfect opportunity for a one-way trip through the country.

If you plan to be in New Zealand for two months or more, a practical option is to buy a used vehicle in Auckland, and then sell it when you leave. You can find a large selection of used vehicles advertised in the Wednesday and Saturday editions of the *NZ Herald* and the *Saturday Star*. Check out the website www.carfair.co.nz for an idea of what is available.

"Car fairs," where owners sell their own vehicles, are held throughout Auckland each weekend. You'll be surprised how many Aucklanders attend—the fairs are almost a social gathering. The largest is at **Ellerslie Racecourse** (Hwy. 1, Greenlane Interchange, 09/529-2233, www.carfair.co.nz, Sun. 9 A.M.–noon). Though not a dealership,

Backpackers Car Market (20 East St., 09/377-7761, www.backpackerscarmarket.co.nz, daily 9:30 A.M.–5 P.M.) is a place where travelers can buy and sell vehicles among themselves. Insurance and inspections are available. It's one block from the top end of Queen Street. **Scotties** (27 New North Rd., 09/303-3912, www.scotties.co.nz) often has former rentals for sale for under $3,000.

By Taxi

The flat charge for a taxi is $3.55, then $2.35 for every kilometer (0.6 mi). Taxis wait outside all major downtown hotels, at the airport, and at the Britomart Transport Centre. Companies include **Auckland Co-op Taxis** (09/300-3000), **Discount Taxis** (09/529-1000), **Hop-a-Cab** (09/355-0000), and **Taxi Combined** (0800/505-550).

Hauraki Gulf Maritime Park

Right on Auckland's back doorstep is an archipelago of 47 islands, spread out over more than 13,600 square km (5,271 sq mi) of Pacific Ocean. The islands are volcanic in origin, some having erupted as recently as 200 years ago. Most of the islands are within Hauraki Gulf Maritime Park and are administered by the Department of Conservation (DOC). Some are simply rocky islets, but a few are inhabited, with bustling little seaside villages. They all have one thing in common—the opportunity for almost unlimited recreation. They are wonderful places to hike, swim, scuba dive, sea kayak, or just visit for a picnic.

Fullers (09/367-9111, www.fullers.co.nz) serves some of the islands with a regular and inexpensive ferry service from the piers in front of the Ferry Building on Quay Street in downtown Auckland. Here you'll find Fullers Cruise Centre, the place to check the ferry schedule, gather island information, and make tour and accommodations bookings. The DOC-operated **Auckland Visitor Centre** (09/379-6476; Mon.–Fri. 9:30 A.M.–5 P.M., Sat. 10 A.M.–3 P.M.), also in the Ferry Building, is a good place to pick up brochures on the islands' human and natural history and to make campground bookings.

RANGITOTO ISLAND

This island, dominating the horizon from along the south shore of Waitemata Harbour,

is easily recognized by its symmetrical and elongated shape. It last erupted only 200 years ago, spreading jagged lava flows out from the peak for a 2.5-km (1.5-mi) radius. Rangitoto has no soil or fresh running water, yet it supports an astonishing array of native and introduced plant species and small colonies of wallaby, deer, and many birds. You can climb to the 259-meter (850-ft) summit for fabulous views by following the walking track from Rangitoto Wharf. If you're walking up (the view is worth the effort!), wear sturdy footwear and take sunscreen and sunglasses—the glare can be intense. Several other walking tracks meander across the island. Another track follows the coast and finishes at Islington Bay, where you can catch the ferry back to downtown instead of backtracking to Rangitoto Wharf. Administered by the DOC, the island is uninhabited, so only day-trippers are permitted.

Getting There

The first of three daily **Fullers** (09/367-9111) ferries departs the Ferry Building at 9:15 A.M. The round-trip fare is adult $27, child $13.50. Walking around the island and to the summit of the volcanic cone is easy, but you can also take the tractor-train **Rangitoto Volcanic Explorer Tour** for an extra adult $32, child $16.

MOTUTAPU ISLAND

Motutapu Island is connected to Rangitoto Island by a natural causeway, yet their types of vegetation are completely different. Traditionally farmland, Motutapu is the subject of an ambitious DOC project to return it to its natural state. The first stage, the eradication of introduced mammals, is complete, and the introduction of endangered species has begun. The project is a long one—50 years at least. The only way to get around the island is on foot. A popular loop begins at the causeway, climbing to the island's highest point before descending to Home Bay. From this point, the trail heads north past scattered World War II gun emplacements before returning along the shoreline to the causeway. This loop is 12 km (7 mi); allow four hours.

Practicalities

The only way to stay overnight on the island is by pitching a tent at **Home Bay Campground** (09/379-6476; $8 per person), a four-km (2.5-mi) walk from the Islington Bay ferry dock on Rangitoto Island. Book through the DOC. **Fullers** (09/367-9111) serves adjacent Rangitoto Island, from where it's a pleasant walk across the causeway to Motutapu.

MOTUIHE ISLAND

A DOC reserve, Motuihe has seen many uses over the years, with local volunteers now doing their best to return the island to its natural state (check www.motuihe.org.nz for volunteer opportunities). Between downtown Auckland and Waiheke Island, Motuihe's biggest attraction is two long white-sand beaches on either side of a narrow isthmus, separated by a band of sand dunes and tall Norfolk pines. One side or the other is always protected from the wind, making it attractive for sailing enthusiasts, beach lovers, and picnickers. Around the coastline lie extensive mudstone reefs, and at low tide the rock pools teem with life. Tracks

take advantage of the numerous natural vantage points offering the most spectacular views. You can walk around the entire island in four hours at low tide.

Practicalities

Discovery 360 (Pier 4, Quay St., 09/307-8005; adult $27, child $17 round-trip) departs three times daily for Motuihe. The last return ferry departs the island at 3:40 P.M. All facilities cluster around Waihaorangatahi Bay (where the ferry docks); they include a kiosk, picnic tables with barbecues, and a campground. For information on camping, or to find out about water taxis serving the island, call the facility operator at 09/534-8095.

◧ WAIHEKE ISLAND

Waiheke Island, second-largest of the gulf islands (92 sq km/36 sq mi), is by far the most populous, with a year-round population of 8,000. This swells fourfold in summer as city slickers swarm over to relax on the beautiful white-sand beaches or to walk through rolling farmland and native bush. The island was settled by Maori 800 years ago, at a time when its rolling inland hills were covered with kauri forests. The kauris, long gone, have been replaced with bustling holiday villages, open farmland, and vineyards.

Sights and Recreation

The island's west end is the most built up, with an almost continuous string of villages extending eastward from the main settlement of **Oneroa** to **Onetangi**. Between the two lies a string of magnificent beaches, including picturesque **Palm Beach.** Hiking trails link all parts of the less-developed eastern end of the island (pick up a detailed description from the local information center), and a pleasant six-km (3.7-mi, two-hour) coastal track links Oneroa with Palm Beach. Return along the same route or jump aboard a bus.

Waiheke's calm waters and convoluted coastline make it ideal for sea kayaking. **Ross**

Adventures (09/372-5550) charges $85 for a range of half-day trips, including one by moonlight. Kayak rentals are from $25 per hour.

At the far end of the island, **Connells Bay Sculpture Park** (Cowes Bay Rd., Connells Bay, 09/372-8957) comprises 25 kinetic sculptures created by some of New Zealand's foremost artists along a sloping hillside with sweeping ocean views. Access is restricted to guests at the Connells Bay lodge and those on a guided tour. These tours depart on demand late October to late April by advance reservation only. The walking tour lasts two hours and costs adult $30, child $15.

Waiheke Museum and Historic Village (Onetangi Rd., Onetangi, 09/372-2970; Wed., and Sat.–Sun. noon–4 P.M.; donation) is small but provides an interesting diversion from more strenuous activities.

Wineries

Waiheke has a reputation for excellent wine, predominantly reds, which thrive in the warm, dry climate. About 25 wineries are spread across the island (Waiheke even has its own winegrowers' association), but most are small, family-run affairs not open to the public. As a general rule, the emphasis is on quality rather than quantity, so you can expect to pay more than in other regions, and most island wineries have adopted a charge for tasting.

The most high-profile winery is **Stonyridge** (Onetangi Rd., 09/372-8822; daily 11:30 A.M.–5 P.M.), whose annual release of Larose—considered one of the world's finest Cabernet blends—is quickly scooped up by connoisseurs the world over, even at $200–300 a bottle. Winery tours depart weekends only at 11:30 A.M. and cost $10, which includes tasting of one red and one white. Almost all Stonyridge wine is sold by mail order; the mailing list is currently oversubscribed, so the only way to taste the wine is by visiting the vineyard. On a high point of land near the ferry dock, the **Mudbrick Vineyard** (126 Church Bay Rd., 09/372-9050; daily 11 A.M.–5 P.M.) is best known for its restaurant and wine bar, but also offers tasting of their well-crafted wines.

Accommodations

The wide range of accommodations can be booked through the island information center (09/372-9999). Accommodations generally are more expensive than those on the mainland, but staying in one of the backpacker lodges reduces costs considerably.

At **Hekerua Lodge** (11 Hekerua Rd., Little Oneroa, 09/372-8990, www.hekerualodge.co.nz, camping $18 per person, dorm bed $30–36, $55 s, $86 d, $120 s or d for an en suite) it's a 600-meter (0.4-mi) walk downhill to the beach from a totally private setting, surrounded by dense native bush. The modern facilities include a wide deck, deep natural-feeling rock swimming pool, bikes, a barbecue, and cozy lounge area with Internet access. (You may hear this place referred to as Waiheke Island Backpackers).

Palm Beach Lodge (23 Tiri View Rd., Palm Beach, 09/372-7763, $280–420 s or d) is a complex of luxurious two-bedroom Mediterranean-style villas, each self-contained and with a private balcony that affords stunning views. Rates include breakfast provisions and use of a variety of facilities.

For understated luxury, nothing on the island comes close to **Connells Bay** (Cowes Bay Rd., Connells Bay, 09/372-8957, www.connellsbay.co.nz, $400 s or d), a beautifully restored 100-year-old cottage just steps from a private beach. The cottage features two bedrooms, a lounge with log fireplace, full kitchen, and verandah with barbecue; you will need to book well in advance to secure a reservation at this highly recommended lodging.

Food

Oneroa has the island's main concentration of eateries. **Vino Vino** (153 Ocean View Rd., Oneroa, 09/372-9888; daily 9 A.M.–10 P.M.; $22–33) is a popular place, both for its great food and elevated ocean views from the covered deck. Favorite dishes are the platters, perfect for sharing, and seafood delights such as the pan-fried scallops. In nearby Ostend, **Nourish** (3 Belgium St., 09/372-3557; daily 8 A.M.–4 P.M.; $12–24) is a modern café that wouldn't look out of place in downtown Auckland. The cooked breakfast was the best I had on the island, while the rest of the day the menu features interesting choices like lamb fillet served on roasted beets.

South of Oneroa, the **Mudbrick Restaurant** (Church Bay Rd., 09/372-9050; daily for lunch and dinner; $44–49) attracts the business crowd from Auckland, who catch a ferry across the bay to enjoy a relaxed lunch among the vines. Evenings are more upscale, but the food and service are equally good, with diners enjoying dishes such as grilled duck breast smothered with a red curry and plum sauce. The winery also offers platters and light meals at the cellar door and an alfresco wine bar with sweeping ocean views that are nothing short of magnificent. **Veranda Cafe** (Stonyridge, Onetangi Rd., 09/372-8822; summer daily 11:30 A.M.–5 P.M.; $23–34) has a modern menu of winery classics (think chilled green pea and coriander soup, carpaccio of Wagyu beef, and an antipasto platter to share).

Information

Waiheke Island Visitor Information Centre (118 Ocean View Rd., Oneroa, 09/372-1234; summer daily 9 A.M.–5 P.M., the rest of the year until 4 P.M.) is a good spot to begin your island adventure. As well as providing information, the center makes accommodation and tour bookings and rents bikes.

Getting There and Around

Many island residents commute to Auckland daily, so sailings are frequent. **Fullers** (09/367-9111, www.fullers.co.nz) ferries depart the downtown Ferry Building up to 20 times daily for the 35-minute trip to the island. Round-trip fares are adult $28.50, senior $25, child $14.30. A number of packages can be booked through Fullers in conjunction with the ferry price. **SeaLink** (09/300-5900 or 0800/732-546, www.sealink.co.nz) offers vehicle and passenger service to the island from Wynyard Wharf, at 45 Jellicoe Street (just west of Viaduct Harbour), on weekends and from Half Moon Bay, east of downtown, daily. Fares are similar; adding a vehicle to the mix costs $142 round-trip.

Once on the island, getting around is easy. The ferry docks at Matiatia Bay, from where buses run along two scheduled routes to all corners of the island. The fare to Oneroa is $1.50 and a day pass is $8.50. **Waiheke Taxi** can be reached at 09/372-8038. **Waiheke Rental Cars** (09/372-8635) has an office beside the wharf at Matiatia Bay; vehicles are $59–89 per day plus 50 cents per km.

GREAT BARRIER ISLAND

Largest of the gulf islands, Great Barrier is also the most remote, lying nearly 100 km (62 mi) from downtown Auckland, but conveniently linked by boat and plane. The island is mostly wilderness, with forested ranges rising more than 600 meters (0.37 mi). Geologically, the island links to the Coromandel Ranges as part of a volcanic fault. The west coast is deeply indented, while many long sandy beaches flank the east coast. The island was first settled by Maori 800 years ago, and its nonrenewable resources, such as kauri forests, were devastated by early Europeans. Today it's a peaceful place, with 1,100 residents scattered mostly over the island's southern end. Recreational opportunities abound—hiking trails crisscross the island, hot springs invite a good soaking, the road system is suited for mountain biking, and the surrounding waters are great for scuba diving and surfing.

Practicalities

Although remote, each of the island's communities offers basic services, such as ATMs and groceries. Accommodations are limited and best booked as part of a package through SeaLink or Fullers. The island has six basic campgrounds, some accessible only on foot. All campers must be totally self-sufficient and prepared with a campstove if a fire ban is in effect. Book campsites through the DOC (09/379-6476; $8 per person per night).

The ferry trip from Auckland with **SeaLink** (09/300-5900 or 0800/732-546, www.sealink.co.nz) takes two hours each way. Departures are once daily from downtown (Wynyard Wharf, 45 Jellicoe St.) and Half Moon Bay. The round-trip fare is adult $120, child $79, vehicle $424. The adult fare to take the ferry one way and return by plane is $169, which makes a day trip possible. **Fullers** (09/367-9111, www.fullers.co.nz) has a summer-only service, with similar fares. **Great Barrier Airlines** (09/256-6500 or 0800/900-600, www.greatbarrierairlines.co.nz) offers scheduled flights between the international airport and the island for $129 each way. **Great Barrier Buses** (09/429-0055) meets all ferry and plane arrivals. You can also rent a vehicle through **GBI Rental Car** (09/429-0062; from $55 per day).

NORTHLAND

North of Auckland lies a spectacular region particularly appealing to sun worshippers, island hoppers, sailors, nature enthusiasts, and history buffs. Apart from a mild climate and plenty of sunshine, the north offers great beauty and variety. The Bay of Islands, where nature and history blend in an unbeatable combination, attracts the largest number of the region's visitors. The irregular 800-km (500-mile) coastline is fringed with soft, sandy beaches and sheltered coves; the bay, formed by a drowned river system, is dotted with some 150 islands. Diving thrills and sensational underwater photography await you in the crystal-clear submarine world of coral reefs and shoals of brightly colored fish, and for excitement, you can't beat a day of deep-sea fishing for the magnificent game fish that cruise the Bay of Islands in abundance. This tropical paradise also lures both overseas and New Zealand sailors, who congregate in the bay gathering supplies, getting repairs, and soaking up the atmosphere, much as the traders and whalers did at the end of the 18th century.

A great deal of New Zealand's notable early history occurred in the north, and throughout the region (particularly in the Bay of Islands) are many well-preserved historic buildings and remains of Maori *pa*. Magnificent Ninety Mile Beach stretches as far as you can see, and if you follow the main road to the end, you come to Cape Reinga, one of the northernmost tips of

© ANDREW HEMPSTEAD

HIGHLIGHTS

© AVALON TRAVEL

LOOK FOR ⟨⟨ TO FIND RECOMMENDED SIGHTS, ACTIVITIES, DINING, AND LODGING.

⟨⟨ **Cruising the Bay of Islands:** Regardless of mainland commercialization, once your tour boat begins wending its way through uninhabited islands you'll be awestruck by the raw beauty of the landscape (page 65).

⟨⟨ **Waitangi Treaty Grounds:** An easily understood approach to explaining New Zealand's most important historic site makes a visit to Waitangi enjoyable. Ocean views and a fantastic little café are a bonus (page 67).

⟨⟨ **Russell:** Captain Cook wouldn't recognize this once-rowdy South Pacific outpost, which is now a quiet haven of upscale accommodations and fine dining (page 71).

⟨⟨ **Kerikeri Basin:** Two of New Zealand's oldest buildings lie side by side in this tranquil riverside location (page 73).

⟨⟨ **Ninety Mile Beach:** Spend a day on the beach—not sun-baking, but driving and "sand surfing"—by joining a guided tour that leads all the way north to Cape Reinga (page 79).

⟨⟨ **Waipoua Forest:** In one of the few places in New Zealand where ancient kauri remain, you can wander through a stand of 1,000-year-old trees and stare upward in wonder (page 84).

⟨⟨ **Kauri Museum:** Once you've walked through Waipoua Forest, stop at this outstanding small-town museum to learn about the industry that almost wiped out the kauri (page 86).

⟨⟨ **Muriwai Beach:** The South Island has most of the country's accessible bird-watching spots, with one exception—this sleepy seaside village where thousands of gannets nest on offshore rock towers (page 87).

New Zealand. See the clashing waves where the Pacific Ocean and Tasman Sea merge. At the southern end of Ninety Mile Beach, several mighty kauri forests still stand. The north is small enough that you can cover it in a few days, but to spend time in its many special places deserves at least a week, especially if your interests include hiking, deep-sea fishing, or diving. Here's hoping you have the time!

PLANNING YOUR TIME

For many visitors, Northland is their first taste of New Zealand driving, and one thing soon becomes apparent—distances are in no way indicative of the time it takes to travel the narrow, winding roads found throughout the country. For example, from Auckland to the Bay of Islands is 237 km (147 mi), but even under the best conditions this trip takes over four hours (and this is on Hwy. 1, the country's main

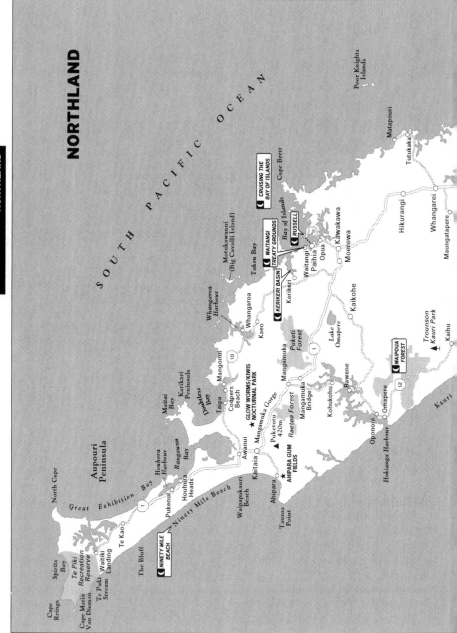

NORTHLAND

SOUTH PACIFIC OCEAN

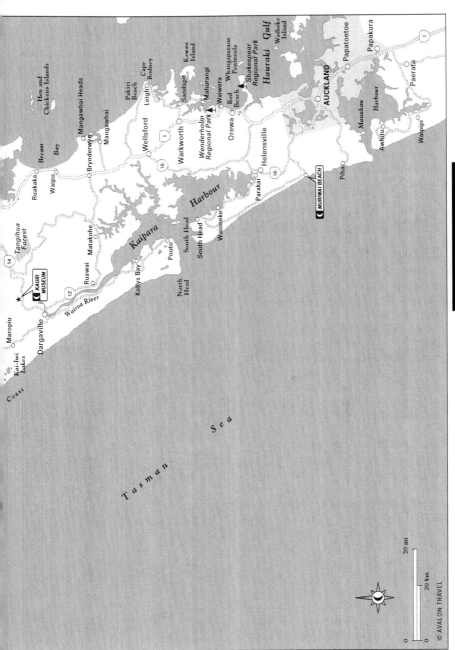

© AVALON TRAVEL

highway). For this reason, in Northland and beyond, it's always important to take note of suggested driving times, rather than just the distance between two points, when planning your time.

If your time in New Zealand is limited to two weeks and you plan on visiting both islands, an overnight trip to Paihia is probably the most sensible option. This would allow time to go **cruising through the Bay of Islands,** step back in time at **Waitangi Treaty Grounds,** and take a ferry trip to **Russell** (heading over for dinner is a popular option).

Three days in Northland allows time to explore the historic buildings of **Kerikeri Basin** and take a tour along **Ninety Mile Beach.** An alternative to the beach tour would be to spend the third day returning to Auckland via the west coast, passing through the giant kauri trees protected by **Waipoua Forest** and stopping by the **Kauri Museum.** Even if you're not a keen bird-watcher, the gannet colony at **Muriwai Beach** is an eye-catching stop, as part of the journey down the west coast or as a half-day trip from Auckland.

Auckland to Whangarei

HIBISCUS COAST

Traveling up Highway 1, you quickly leave the suburbs behind and get a first taste of rural New Zealand: rich agricultural land, lush green fields, grazing sheep and cows. Greenhouses and nurseries line the roads in some areas, and roadside stalls sell fresh fruit and vegetables at good prices. The town of Silverdale, only 40 km from Auckland, marks the beginning of the Hibiscus Coast, which includes Whangaparaoa (Bay of Whales) Peninsula and stretches as far north as Hatfields Beach.

Shakespear Regional Park

At the eastern tip of the Whangaparaoa Peninsula, this park offers good bush and farm walks, as well as three sandy beaches safe for swimming. If you're in the area on a windy day, head for the steep cliffs near Army Bay and check out the hang-glider action. Another popular activity is shellfishing, good at low tide; place the shellfish on a barbecue and cook them until they open.

Red Beach

If you're an early riser, head for this beach before it gets light—it's spectacular at sunrise. The wet orange shells left by the receding tide reflect the

sun's rays, and the entire beach takes on a red glow. Adding to the beauty are the native flax flowers and *pohutukawa* trees (covered in bright scarlet flowers at Christmas) at the southern end. The beach offers safe swimming, surf suitable

© ANDREW HEMPSTEAD

Shakespear Regional Park

TRAVELING NORTH FROM AUCKLAND

Two main highways lead north from Auckland. The faster and more direct is Highway 1, which crosses Waitemata Harbour via Auckland Harbour Bridge, then passes through Warkworth, Wellsford, and Whangarei before reaching the Bay of Islands and Kaitaia. The alternate route is Highway 16 (called the North Western Motorway within city limits), along the west coast through Muriwai Beach and Helensville. This highway rejoins Highway 1 at Wellsford, then branches west again as Highway 16 on the north side of Kaipara Harbour, closely following the west coast north via Dargaville.

BY BUS

Intercity (09/623-1503, www.intercity.co.nz) runs several coaches a day from Auckland to Kaitaia via Whangarei and Paihia, the gateway to the Bay of Islands. Intercity departs from the SkyCity Coach Terminal (102 Hobson St.) in downtown Auckland.

---

for beginners, lifeguard patrol on weekends and holidays, and short rock walks at either end.

Orewa Beach

Since being bypassed by Highway 1 in 2007, the beachside suburb of Orewa, 30 km (19 mi) north of downtown, has become a bit quieter, but the long stretch of white sand is still popular (beware of the strong rip where the Orewa River meets the sea; on weekends and holidays it's patrolled by local surf club members). At the northern end you can see the remains of an ancient Maori *pa* site on the hilltop above Orewa House, and at the extreme north, over Grut's Bridge and sharply to the left, lies the entrance to **Eaves Bush**. This small reserve contains some impressive kauri trees and lots of native ferns.

Pillows Travellers Lodge (412 Hibiscus Coast Hwy., 09/426-6338, www.pillows.co.nz,

dorm beds $25, $50–65 s or d) is one of the many accommodations in New Zealand built specifically to cater to backpackers. You'll find a comfortable lounge, kitchen, laundry, sundeck, inner courtyard filled with greenery, and public Internet access.

⬤ Waves (Kohu St., 09/427-0888 or 0800/426-6889, www.waves.co.nz, $185–285 s or d), within a block of the beach, has a resort-like atmosphere and 20 modern, practical rooms filled with amenities such as luxurious bathrooms and modern kitchens. Upgrade to a premium room and enjoy extras such as a large-screen TV, wireless Internet, and bathrobes.

Waiwera

Waiwera is a thermal resort and busy tourist area. If relaxing in hot pools sounds appealing, follow the signs from the highway to **Waiwera Thermal** (09/427-8800; Sun.–Thurs. 9 A.M.–9 P.M., Fri.–Sat. 9 A.M.–10 P.M.; adult $26, senior $10, child $15), nestled behind a beach at the mouth of a river. The 26 indoor and outdoor pools vary in temperature 28–43°C (82–109°F), and there are private spas, water slides, a waterfall pool, a movie pool where the latest releases are shown on a big screen, picnic areas, and a food kiosk. Private spas are $50 per person for one hour, which includes general admission.

KOWHAI COAST

The Kowhai Coast stretches from Wenderholm Regional Park in the south to Pakiri Beach in the north. In between, the mighty Mahurangi River estuary has forged its way inland, allowing easy boat access to Warkworth, the main town on this stretch of coast.

Waiwera to Warkworth

Bush and beach trails offer good hiking in **Wenderholm Regional Park** (State Hwy. 1, www.arc.govt.nz), a beautiful reserve where birdlife is prolific and the wide sandy beach is

© ANDREW HEMPSTEAD

Waves is a laidback accommodation perfectly suited to the beachside ambiance of Orewa.

perfect for a leisurely stroll. Behind the beach is an open coastal forest dotted with picnic tables. Historic Couldrey House is open for inspection on weekends. The park is open in summer daily 6 A.M.–9 P.M., the rest of the year daily 6 A.M.–7 P.M. Camping is $10 per person.

Pohuehue Scenic Reserve, off Highway 1, is another enjoyable place for hiking. Signposted walkways lead through a spectacular variety of native trees, ferns, and exotic plants. **Moir Hill Walkway** also starts on Highway 1, six km (four mi) south of Warkworth; it will take you 3.5 hours to walk the six-km trail (five to six hours round-trip). The path climbs through the trees, drops to a stream and waterfall, and again climbs to Moir Hill lookout, where great views of Hauraki Gulf await you. As an alternate return route, the track meanders back through Pohuehue Scenic Reserve.

The **Honey Centre** (7 Perry Rd., 09/425-8003; daily 8:30 A.M.–5 P.M.; free) is beside Highway 3, 20 kilometers north of Orewa. It

has the country's largest bee observatory; visitors can view tens of thousands of bees hard at work making honey. There's free honey tasting and, naturally, a gift shop stocked with a wide variety of honey-related products, including royal jelly.

WARKWORTH AND VICINITY

Many small family orchards grow to the south of this charming fishing village along the upper tidal reaches of the Mahurangi River (freshly picked fruit—cheaper than in town—beckons from roadside stalls), which has colonial-style architecture and numerous cafés and restaurants. Warkworth (pop. 3,400) is the main town between Auckland, 70 km (43 mi) south, and Whangarei, and well worth a side trip off the main highway before you continue north.

SheepWorld Farm & Nature Park (09/425-7444; adult $26, senior $22, child $10) lies four km (2.5 mi) north of town along Highway 1. The highlight of a visit is the Dog & Sheep

Show (daily at 11 A.M. and 2 P.M.), which includes sheepshearing, dogs demonstrating their roundup skills, and the opportunity to bottle-feed baby lambs. Part of the four-hectare (10-acre) complex is the Black Sheep Café, with lots of outdoor tables, a country-style store stocked with a huge collection of wool and sheepskin products, and a small petting zoo.

As early as the 1860s, Nathaniel Wilson and his sons began to manufacture the first "Portland Cement" made in New Zealand. Abandoned in 1929, the ruins of the **Wilson Cement Works** (Wilson Rd.) are open to the public, with the riverside site popular for swimming and a grassed area shaded by trees a good picnic spot.

Warkworth and District Museum

Inside this surprisingly large museum (Tudor Collins Dr., 09/425-7093; summer daily 9 A.M.–4 P.M., the rest of the year 9 A.M.–3 P.M.; adult $8, child $2) you'll find

Warkworth is along the Mahurangi River.

© ANDREW HEMPSTEAD

stacks of information on local history, and every nook and cranny is crammed with useful objects and curios from the past. Outside is a beautiful half-hectare (one-acre) park containing fine kauri trees—check out the two giant ones near the museum. The McKinney Kauri is 800 years old, and reaches a mere 11.89 meters (39 ft) at the first limb. The museum is accessed from the south end of town; take McKinney Road off Highway 1, turn right on Thompson Road, and follow signs.

Practicalities

Within walking distance of downtown and the river is **Walton Park Motor Lodge** (2 Walton Ave., 09/425-8149, www.waltonpark.co.nz, $115–210 s or d), where each of the spacious units has basic cooking facilities, including a microwave. Other facilities include a swimming pool, a guest laundry, and a restaurant offering delicious char-grilled dishes ($24–34).

Take the road to Snells Beach from Warkworth and you'll eventually come to the appealing whitewashed homestead of **Mahurangi Lodge** (416 Mahurangi East Rd., 09/425-5465, www.pacificviewslodge.co.nz, $65–75 s, $85–105 d). The bed-and-breakfast, perched atop a small hill, has a sweeping verandah with great views of the surrounding lush countryside and distant ocean beaches. The two least expensive guest rooms (there are four rooms total) share a bathroom. The lodge is located about 11 km (seven mi) from Warkworth.

In a rural setting above Snells Beach, the faux Tudor **Salty Dog Inn** (09/425-5588, www.saltydoginn.co.nz, $120–210 s or d) provides 14 spacious and modern units, each with a king-size bed and writing desk. The in-house restaurant (daily for dinner; $16–26) offers a creative menu of innovative dishes, such as Cajun salmon kebabs for a starter, followed by slow-roasted lamb shank for a main.

Park by the river in downtown Warkworth, where you'll find a number of good little cafés

NORTHLAND

close by. My favorite of these is **Farmhouse Café** (4 Kapanui St., 09/425-9940; daily 8 A.M.–4 P.M.; $8–15), which has a homely ambience and alfresco riverside dining surrounded by lush greenery. A few shops uphill from the river, **Sea Food N Eat It** (7 Neville St., 09/425-7005; daily from 11 A.M.; $8–13) serves up takeout fish and chips—perfect for a riverside picnic.

Warkworth Information Centre (1 Baxter St., 09/425-9081, www.warkworthnz.com; Mon.–Fri. 8:30 A.M.–5 P.M., Sat.–Sun. 9 A.M.–3 P.M.) is beside the river at the end of the main street.

KAWAU ISLAND

Sandspit Wharf, 6.5 km (four mi) from Warkworth, is the place to catch ferries and cruise boats to Kawau Island, a delightful spot with 300 residents and a number of sandy beaches. The island was the home of Sir George Grey, governor of New Zealand 1845–1853 and 1861–1867. His residence, elegant **Mansion House,** has been restored to its former glory. Of particular note is the surrounding garden, which is filled with exotic species collected by Grey from around the world. Although most of the island is privately owned, you can walk across the lush farmland, discover small sheltered bays, and take in all the wildlife. Along with many bird species, four species of wallaby introduced by Sir Grey in 1870 continue to dominate the animal life. At the historic home, **Mansion House Café** (09/422-8903) is open for lunch through the summer holidays, but the island has no other services.

Kawau Water Taxis (09/425-8006 or 0800/111-616; adult $50, child $26) has regular ferries departing from Sandspit four times daily throughout summer, taking 50 minutes to reach Mansion House Bay.

WARKWORTH TO WHANGAREI
Dome Forest Walkway

This track, signposted on Highway 1 between Warkworth and Wellsford, climbs through Dome Forest to the Dome, a flat-topped mountain. At 336 meters (1,102 ft) it's one of the highest peaks in the area, and has great views of Hauraki Gulf. The path to the summit starts beside a roadside café and takes about 40 minutes; on to Waiwhiu Kauri Grove takes another 30 minutes. The path is well marked (look for the white markings on the tree trunks). Steps have been cut in the steepest sections, but the track itself remains quite steep and gets pretty slippery when wet. Ascend to Highway 1 along the same route.

A Coastal Detour: Leigh and Pakiri Beach

As an alternative to Highway 1 north from Warkworth, consider taking a detour east through Leigh and Pakiri Beach, rejoining the highway at Wellsford. Eight km (five mi) from the highway, Takatu Road spurs southeast along the **Takatu Peninsula.**

Along the way, the understated luxury of **Sandpiper Lodge** (841 Takatu Rd., 09/422-7256, www.sandpiperlodge.co.nz, $400–495 s or d) makes for a wonderful overnight stop. Set on a two-hectare (five-acre) property on an estuary, it features a pool surrounded by native gardens, a restaurant, and a bar/lounge. Rooms in the main lodge open to the pool and gardens while the larger, more private chalets lie right on the estuary. Rates include breakfast; dinner is an additional $65 per person.

Facing the open ocean, Pakiri Beach is a long, white sandy beach. **Pakiri Beach Holiday Park** (Rakiri River Rd., 09/422-6199, www.pakiriholidaypark.co.nz, camping $30, cabins from $60) has a beachfront location with a barbecue area, modern kitchen, and games room. The least expensive self-contained cottages are $110 s or d; a beachfront cottage is $175.

North from Wellsford

At **Mangawhai Heads,** a small resort town north of Wellsford, you'll find the head of a two-hour walk along the cliffs that provides spectacular views of the offshore islands. From Mangawhai Heads, the road continues north to **Waipu Cove Beach,** popular for fishing and swimming, and rejoins Highway 1 at **Waipu.**

Continuing north, not far from Ruakaka, is the turnoff to **Marsden Point Oil Refinery,** New Zealand's only oil refinery, which refines crude oil shipped in from the Middle East. Naturally, visitors may not enter the refinery, but from the top of Pilbrow's Hill (to the south of Waipu) you can clearly see its flare. At the Visitors Centre (Marsden Point Rd., Ruakaka, 09/432-8194; daily 10 A.M.–5 P.M.; free), adjacent to the main entrance, you can view an intricate model of the refinery and a documentary.

Whangarei and Vicinity

Whangarei (pop. 46,000), 130 km (81 mi) north of Warkworth and 70 km (44 mi) south of Paihia, stands alone as the only city in Northland. Founded on the edge of an extremely deep and sheltered harbor, it quickly became a thriving port. To the Maori, the harbor was known as Teranga Paraoa (Where the Whales Run). Today the harbor is a mecca for yachties from around the world—many of the brochures describe the city as the "International Yachting Centre of the North Island." Whangarei's mild climate boasts about 2,000 sunshine hours a year, 1,600 mm (63 in) of rain, and temperatures ranging from 6° to 28°C (43–82°F) throughout the year—the average temperature is 19°C (66°F).

SIGHTS AND RECREATION
Town Basin Marina

A few blocks from downtown, Town Basin Marina is the tie-up point for yachts from around the world, which sail up the Hatea River to Whangarei and one of New Zealand's best deepwater anchorages. An area on the basin's south side has been landscaped with gardens, and paved walkways wind through gift shops, boutiques, and cafés with outdoor eating areas. An intriguing museum at the basin is **Claphams Clocks** (09/483-3993; daily 10 A.M.–5 P.M.; adult $8, senior $6, child $4), featuring an assortment of nearly 1,000 clocks and watches contributed by Mr. A. Clapham, who made many of them himself. In the courtyard out front is Australasia's largest sundial, with an interpretive panel describing how it works.

Along the river from the main concentration of shops is **Reyburn House** (Quay St., 09/438-3074; Tues.–Fri. 10 A.M.–4 P.M., Sat.–Sun. 1–4 P.M.; free), a kauri home dating to 1865 and now home to a gallery featuring the work of local artists.

Whangarei Museum and Heritage Park

This excellent museum (09/438-9630; daily 10 A.M.–4 P.M.; adult $10, child $5) is just a small part of a large complex that comprises a kiwi house, an old homestead, and 25-hectare (62-acre) grounds laced with hiking trails that lead to a stream and various waterfalls. The museum itself has a large number of Maori and European artifacts collected from throughout Northland, while **Clarke Homestead,** built in 1885, has been restored, with many of the rooms furnished as they would have been in that era. In the kiwi house, the natural cycle of day and night has been reversed so that visitors can watch these intriguing nocturnal creatures feeding and moving around at a decent hour. During the summer, local volunteers put on "live days" every second Sunday, operating a steam engine and antique farm equipment. It's on Highway 14, four km (2.5 mi) west of Whangarei—follow signs out of town to Dargaville.

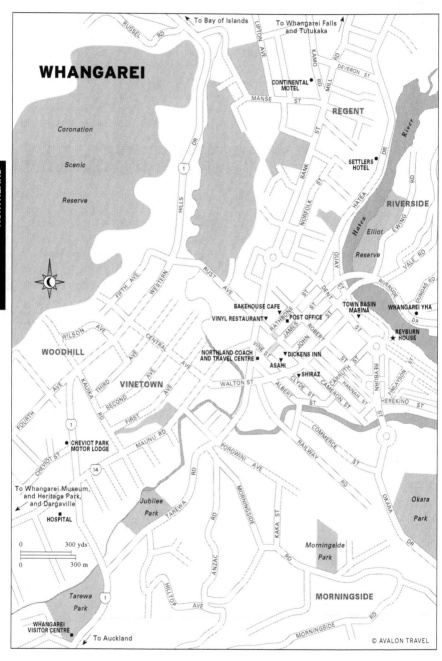

To Bay of Islands

To Whangarei Falls
and Tutukaka

WHANGAREI

RUSSEL RD

LIPTON AVE

KAMO RD

MILL

DEVERON ST

CONTINENTAL
MOTEL

MANSE ST

ST

REGENT

BANK ST

DR

HATEA

River

Coronation

Scenic

Reserve

HILLS DR

1

SETTLERS
HOTEL

NORFOLK ST

QUAY

Hatea

RIVERSIDE

EWING RD

Elliot

Reserve

VALE RD

DUNDAS RD

FIFTH AVE

WESTERN

RUST AVE

RIVERSIDE DR

ST

DENT ST

ST

BAKEHOUSE CAFE

TOWN BASIN
MARINA

WHANGAREI YHA

WILSON AVE

CENTRAL AVE

VINYL RESTAURANT

RATHBONE ST

JAMES ST

POST OFFICE

ROBERT ST

ST

REYBURN
HOUSE

REYBURN ST

WOODHILL

AVE

KAUKA RD

THIRD AVE

SECOND

AVE

VINE ST

NORTHLAND COACH
AND TRAVEL CENTRE

ASAHI

JOHN ST

DICKENS INN

SHIRAZ

CARRUTH ST

HANNAH ST

FINLAYSON

HEREKINO ST

VINETOWN

FIRST

WALTON ST

ALBERT ST

CLYDE ST

CAMERON ST

FOURTH AVE

CHEVIOT PARK
MOTOR LODGE

MAUNU RD

POROWINI AVE

RAILWAY

COMMERCE ST

CHEVIOT ST

14

RD

MORNINGSIDE RD

OKARA DR

To Whangarei Museum,
and Heritage Park,
and Dargaville

*Jubilee
Park*

TAREWA RD

RD

KAKA ST

*Okara
Park*

HOSPITAL

ANZAC

*Morningside
Park*

0   300 yds

0   300 m

HILLTOP AVE

*Tarewa
Park*

1

MORNINGSIDE

WHANGAREI
VISITOR CENTRE

To Auckland

MORNINGSIDE RD

© AVALON TRAVEL

Claphams Clocks

Whangarei Falls

These falls are a photographer's dream. They drop 26 meters (85 ft) into a deep green pool surrounded by bush, and numerous walkways allow views from above and below. A lookout is just below the main parking lot, or you can take the one-km (0.6-mi) trail that descends to the valley floor below the falls and then loops back around the far side of the river. On a hot summer day, the upper swimming hole, directly above the falls, is a hive of activity. Local children swing out on tree ropes, or dive from the top limbs of a tree into one of the deep holes, entertaining visitors with their audacity. Look for the falls on the outskirts of Whangarei in the suburb of Tikipunga, next to Ngunguru Road (buses run from downtown to Tikipunga).

Tutukaka and Vicinity

Thirty km (19 mi) beyond Whangarei Falls, the road emerges at a beautiful stretch of the northern coastline. **Ngunguru,** the first town along the route, sits on the edge of the Ngunguru River. A sandy beach, lots of swimming and boating action, and many holiday homes give Ngunguru its vacation atmosphere.

Tutukaka is the hub for deep-sea fishing and diving. The **Tutukaka Club,** an arm of the Whangarei Deep Sea Anglers Club based at Tutukaka Marina (09/434-3818, www.sportfishing.co.nz), provides all the information on local fishing, diving, cruising, and boat chartering. The season for catching marlin, shark, or yellowtail tuna usually runs from mid-January through April, no license required. Charter boats cost $700–1,000 per day. If you're by yourself, the club tries to hook you up with a group, lowering the cost to as little as $200 per person. Line fishing, as part of a group, costs about $70 per person per day. For spectacular views of the coastline with its irresistible bays, colorful sailing boats, and shell-studded beaches, follow Tutukaka Block Road up to Tutukaka Heads.

Continuing north, the holiday town of **Matapouri** has a long, white sandy beach, calm water (perfect for swimming and snorkeling), and several other small and more private beaches—reached by wading around the rocks at the northern end. At the back of the third small beach you'll find a trail (take shoes or sandals) that passes through a rock tunnel to emerge at a beautiful cove with good snorkeling potential. Sometimes in summer the waters off Matapouri Beach become thick with plankton; local swimmers don't seem to mind, but it's a rare and unforgettable sensation to swim unexpectedly into the thick, jellylike substance when the water appears to be clear.

Around the next headland is **Sandy Bay.** Keep your eyes peeled for the lookout and great views at Whale Bay Reserve. An easily followed cliffside trail leads from the lookout to the right. Passing through exotic natural bush and groves of *pohutukawa* trees, the trail leads down the cliffs and emerges at beautiful Whale Bay Beach. The walk from the car park to this

NORTHLAND

© ANDREW HEMPSTEAD

Whangarei Falls

fairly isolated beach takes about 20 minutes, but if you suffer from hay-fever allergies, this walk can be miserable in summer. After passing the road to Sandy Bay (known for good surfing—it usually boasts surfable waves when none of the other beaches do), the road swoops back inland toward Hikurangi, where it rejoins Highway 1, 18 km (11 mi) north of Whangarei.

Hiking

Several scenic reserves dot the Whangarei area. **Parahaki Scenic Reserve** contains Parahaki Mountain, with good bush walks and great views of Whangarei from its 241-meter (791-ft) summit. Two of the clearly marked walks originate from Mair Park, at the western foot of Parahaki, the third from Dundas Road at the southern foot. All converge at the summit, where the tall column of the Parahaki War Memorial stands. Ross Track features a gold mine near the summit and a waterfall near the base. About a 10-minute walk from Dundas

Road (close to the Whangarei Hostel), the track takes about 40 minutes each way. Drummond Track takes about the same time to complete—it's pretty steep and features a giant kauri tree along a short sidetrack, one-third of the way down. Dobbie Track starts at Dobbie Park and takes about 50 minutes to the summit, featuring many varied views of Whangarei. On all the walks, Maori pits and old gum-digging workings add to the scenery. Regenerating kauri trees and a variety of ferns (from the tiny crepe and kidney ferns to the large tree ferns) abound along the tracks. Pick up the free *Whangarei Walks* pamphlet—a guide to Scenic Reserves and Walkways in the Whangarei district, available from Whangarei Visitor Centre (92 Otaika Rd., Tarewa Park, 09/438-1079, www.whangareinz.com, Mon.–Fri. 8:30 A.M.–5 P.M., Sat.–Sun. 9:30 A.M.–4:30 P.M.).

A. H. Reed Memorial Kauri Park, in the suburb of Tikipunga about five km (three mi) from downtown next to Whareora Road, is an appealing little park with a variety of trees and a choice of several paths; see the surviving remnant of a kauri forest, Wai Koromiko Stream, and a waterfall.

ACCOMMODATIONS AND CAMPING

Whangarei has about 20 hotels and motels, most of which lie along the main highway through town. The least expensive rooms start at about $80, but for a few extra bucks, there are several really nice places to stay.

Under $50

The small **Whangarei YHA** (52 Punga Grove Ave., 09/438-8954, www.yha.co.nz, dorm beds $24, twin $26) is centrally located on a hill overlooking the Hatea River and an easy five-minute walk from Town Basin. The hostel has only 27 beds, but facilities are good, including a pleasant outdoor area with a barbecue. The hosts rent bicycles and can show the way to all the local attractions.

Whangarei Falls Holiday Park (Whangarei-Tutukaka Rd., 09/437-0609 or 0800/227-222, www.whangareifalls.co.nz) is a pleasant 200-meter (656-ft) walk from Whangarei Falls, about five km (3.1 mi) northeast of town. Tent and caravan sites are $13 per person. Heated cabins cost from $20 s or d. Enjoy the spa or small outdoor pool, participate in the barbecues held on some summer nights, and check your Internet at the front-desk terminal.

$50-100

The **Continental Motel** (67 Kamo Rd., 09/437-6359 or 0800/457-634, www.continentalmotel.co.nz, $80–100 s or d) offers less expensive rates than the town's other motels and a swimming pool to complement 16 spacious units.

$100-150

Cheviot Park Motor Lodge (corner of Western Hills Dr. and Cheviot St., 09/438-2341 or 0508/243-846, www.cheviot-park.co.nz, $100–130 s or d) features 15 slightly-better-than-standard units, each with a kitchen, as well as a pool, spa, and barbecue area. And although it's on the main road, a high fence surrounds the property, affording privacy. Breakfast can be delivered to your room and a dining room opens for dinner Monday–Thursday.

Another choice just out of town is the **Settlers Hotel** (61 Hatea Dr., 09/438-2699 or 0800/666-662, www.settlershotel.co.nz, $70–140 s, $100–140 d), set among exotic gardens beside the Hatea River. The least expensive rooms are older, but the pool, patio, and barbecue area are nice touches. The in-house restaurant is open daily for breakfast and dinner, and for a Sunday brunch popular with the locals.

$150-200

If you feel like a splurge and fancy a self-contained unit with either a fantastic ocean or harbor view and use of a pool, spa, and private beach, head for **☕ Pacific Rendezvous** (09/434-3847 or 0800/999-800, www.oceanresort.co.nz), spread over a high headland at Tutukaka, 29 km (18 mi) from Whangarei. This stretch of coast holds many accommodations, but this is by far the best. Rates range from $165 for a one-bedroom unit to $220 for a three-bedroom unit with ocean views. All are fully self-contained; other resort features include a tennis court and putting green. To get there from Whangarei, drive two km (one mi) beyond Ngunguru, take the Tutukaka Block Road, then turn onto Motel Road and follow it to the end.

FOOD

You'll find many cafés offering good lunches and snacks at any time of the day throughout downtown.

For an inexpensive, no-frills cooked breakfast, make your way downtown to the **Bakehouse Cafe** (21 Rathbone St., 09/438-8188; Mon.–Sat. 7 A.M.–4:30 P.M.). The rest of the day, toasted sandwiches are from $3 and burgers max out at $6. A couple of doors up is **Hills Whangarei Café** (13 Rathbone St., 09/438-8761; Mon.–Fri. 7 A.M.–3 P.M., Sat. 8 A.M.–5 P.M.), a step up in style and substance, with breakfasts such as strawberry pancakes topped with chocolate sauce ($12) and lunches that include lamb salad with papadums ($15).

Dickens Inn (corner of Cameron St. and Quality St. Mall, 09/430-0406; daily from 8 A.M.) is a Tudor-style English restaurant with a number of dining areas. The menu offers no real surprises—instead you get hearty home-style cooking in a welcoming atmosphere. The side of the Dickens Inn opens to a cobbled walkway where you'll find **Café Paparazzi** (Quality St. Mall, 09/438-2961; Mon.–Sat. 8 A.M.–4 P.M.), a Mediterranean-style café where the outdoor tables are covered by large umbrellas and the walls adorned by colorful murals. It'll cost about $20 for the salmon and prosciutto Caesar salad with a honey and banana smoothie on the side. At the back of the walkway beside the Dickens Inn, the modern look of **Asahi** (corner of Vine and Quality Sts., 09/430-3005; daily 11 A.M.–3 P.M. and from 5 P.M.) belies an inexpensive and traditional menu of Japanese favorites.

A couple of blocks east of the main downtown concentration of eateries, **Shiraz** (58 Walton St., 09/438-3112; Mon.–Sat. 11 A.M.–2 P.M., daily from 5 P.M.; $16–22) is a bright space filled with the smells of traditional Indian cooking.

A number of stylish eateries can be found beside **Town Basin Marina,** overlooking a harbor and surrounded by landscaped gardens. Here, **Reva's on the Waterfront** (Town Basin Marina, 31 Quayside, 09/438-8969; daily 10:30 A.M.–9:30 P.M.; $18–31) commands fine harbor views, especially the tables along the verandah. The blackboard menu features pizza, salads, and seafood dishes.

Downtown, **Vinyl Restaurant** (Vale Rd., 09/438-8105; Mon.–Fri. 11:30 A.M.–9 P.M.; Sat. 8 A.M.–9 P.M., Sun. 9 A.M.–9 P.M.; $29–35)

offers something for all tastes and budgets (think Asian glazed pork belly or prosciutto-wrapped fish) in a welcoming atmosphere.

INFORMATION AND SERVICES

As you enter town from the south on Highway 1, make a stop at **Whangarei Visitor Centre** (92 Otaika Rd., Tarewa Park, 09/438-1079, www.whangareinz.com, Mon.–Fri. 8:30 A.M.–5 P.M., Sat.–Sun. 9:30 A.M.–4:30 P.M.). The center has an interesting little gift shop and a café.

Whangarei's main post office is at 16 Rathbone Street. **James St. Laundromat** (66 James St., 09/430-0520) is in the heart of downtown.

Whangarei Area Hospital (09/430-4100) is on Hospital Road. **Primecare Medical Centre** (12 Kensington Ave., 09/437-9070) has a doctor on duty 24 hours daily. Next door is **Kensington Pharmacy** (09/437-3722).

GETTING THERE AND AROUND

It's a short 35-minute hop with **Air New Zealand** (0800/800-737, www.airnewzealand.com) from Auckland to Whangarei, but as the Auckland airport is on the south side of the city and it's only a 2.5-hour drive from downtown, flying is not that practical. **Northland Coach and Travel Centre** (3 Bank St., 09/438-3206) is a stop for **Intercity** (09/438-2653, www.intercity.co.nz) buses.

Whangarei Bus (09/438-6005) charges $3–4 per sector along routes that fan out from Rose Street (by the Grand Hotel) to the suburbs and Whangarei Falls. The main car rental agencies in Whangarei are **Avis** (09/438-2929), **Budget** (09/438-7292), and **Hertz** (09/438-9790). Local taxis are operated by **Kiwi Cabs** (09/420-2299).

WHANGAREI TO THE BAY OF ISLANDS

From Whangarei, it's 70 km (44 mi) north to Paihia, gateway to the Bay of Islands.

To Paihia or Russell

At Kawakawa, Highway 10 spurs northeast to

Paihia and the Bay of Islands. If you're traveling by vehicle, it's best to decide whether to stay in Paihia or Russell before you get to Opua, where the vehicular ferry departs for Russell. It's less hassle and cheaper to leave the car in Paihia, and the passenger ferry across to Russell is short, enjoyable, and frequent. Many of the attractions in Russell are within walking distance of the ferry. However, if you want to explore Russell by road, the car ferry leaves from Opua (a 15-minute drive south of Paihia) and crosses the Veronica Channel to Okiato, from where Russell is a 10-minute drive to the north. The trip costs $10 one-way per vehicle and driver, plus $1 per passenger. The service runs daily 7 A.M.–9 P.M. It's also possible to drive all the way from Highway 1 to Russell, avoiding the ferry altogether; but the access road, which spurs off Highway 1 at Whakapara, is unpaved, winding, and very slow going.

Bay of Islands

The Bay of Islands is one of New Zealand's most beautiful and historic areas. Situated 257 km (160 mi) north of Auckland (allow five hours by road), its irregular coastline and 144 islands are lapped by warm aquamarine waters and bathed in sunshine year-round. The mild climate of the "Winterless North" and the calm waters have made the area a sailor's paradise ever since its discovery by Captain James Cook in the 18th century. Quiet coves, soft sandy beaches, sparkling waters, and island groves of *pohutukawa* trees abound. For excitement there's the challenge of deep-sea fishing for a magnificent marlin or shark, or the chance to dive into a colorful submarine habitat.

The main population center is **Paihia,** 70 km (44 mi) north of Whangarei and the base for cruises and fishing and diving trips, as well as a large number of accommodations and restaurants. Nearby is **Waitangi,** historically important for the signing of the Treaty of Waitangi. Across the bay from Paihia is **Russell.** This delightful village is on the mainland, but road access is roundabout; most visitors arrive by passenger ferry from Paihia. **Kerikeri,** a citrus center and home to many artists and craftspeople, is a short drive from Paihia.

History

Captain Cook named the Bay of Islands in 1769. At that time, it was inhabited by a large Maori population, whose *pa* (fortified dwellings) studded the bay. Captain Cook's ship, the *Endeavour,* was met by a small fleet of canoes navigated by fearless warriors who came to gaze in astonishment at the huge "winged canoe." The first meeting between Europeans and Maori was friendly; however, this changed three years later when a series of blunders by the French explorer Marion Du Fresne led to his murder by the local tribe, and in retaliation some 250 Maori were slain.

By the end of the 18th century, the Bay of Islands had become a thriving trade center, with the whalers, timber-seekers, and traders calling in at Kororareka (present-day Russell) for supplies as well as the proverbial wine, women, and song. The migratory path of whales, unfortunately close to the northern coastline, contributed to their plunder. The tall, straight kauri trees that fringed the bay and lowlands were quickly depleted for ship masts or export to Sydney. Traders also brought predators, disease, and massive exploitation to New Zealand. In the early 19th century many missionaries arrived, and their Christian influence helped end Maori warfare.

There was considerable foreign interest in New Zealand by 1831 and, in fear of takeover, a group of local Maori chiefs asked Britain for

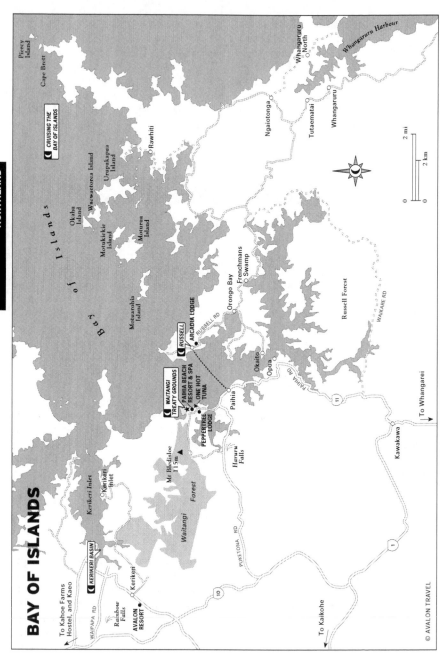

NORTHLAND

BAY OF ISLANDS

© AVALON TRAVEL

BAY OF ISLANDS MARITIME AND HISTORIC PARK

This mostly undeveloped park, comprising about 40 sites scattered throughout the Bay of Islands, protects both scenic and historic areas. The exception to this noncommercial paradise is **Urupukapuka Island,** where Fullers GreatSights (0800/653-339, www.dolphincruises.co.nz) makes a regular stop on most of its cruises. A seven-km (4.3-mi), three-hour hiking trail roughly circles the otherwise untainted island, passing secluded beaches, archeological sites, and several campgrounds.

Cape Brett (Rakaumangamanga) scenic reserve was named by Captain Cook. A 17.5-km (11-mi) track, starting at Oke Bay on Rawhiti Road, takes seven to eight hours. Classified as a hard tramp, it's recommended only for those with above-average fitness and experience (sea access is possible in calm conditions). The old lighthouse on the point was built in 1909, and the lighthouse keeper's cottage has been converted into a hut that can sleep 12, with toilet and water.

Motukawanui (Big Cavalli Island) is a large island reserve, known for its scenic track (1.5 hours) covering the length of the island. The island hut has eight bunks, a toilet, and fresh water.

Impressive **Ranfurly Bay Reserve,** at the entrance to Whangaroa Harbour, is known for rugged volcanic rock formations. The Ranfurly Bay hut provides 12 bunks, toilets, and water, and deepwater anchorage in the bay. You can hike three well-marked tracks from the bay, each providing outstanding harbor views.

PARK PRACTICALITIES

The only practical way to travel to and around the park is by boat. Many cruises visit the more popular spots, such as Urupukapuka Island and Cape Brett, with Fullers GreatSights offering the option of spending a full day on Urupukapuka.

The best source of park information is the **Russell Visitor Centre** (The Strand, Russell, 09/407-0300; summer daily 9 A.M.-5 P.M., the rest of the year Mon.-Fri. 9 A.M.-4:30 P.M.), where you'll find interesting displays and an excellent audiovisual on New Zealand's early history. The staff provides hordes of information (including the brochure Bay of Islands Walks), issues camping and hut permits, and offers a list of charter operators.

NORTHLAND

protection. In February 1840, with the ceremonial signing of the Treaty of Waitangi, New Zealand became a British colony. Within the next year, New Zealand's "capital" was set up at Okiato and named Russell, but it was soon decided that the capital should be moved to the more desirable site of Auckland. The name Russell was then transferred to the town of Kororareka, in hopes that the new name would give the "Hellhole of the Pacific" a new image.

RECREATION

The *real* Bay of Islands—a remote ocean wilderness accessible only by water—is beyond the region's main towns of Paihia, Russell, and Kerikeri. Along with all the services you'll need for an overnight stay, these three towns each have their own charm.

Cruising the Bay of Islands

Most day trips depart from in front of the Maritime Building in Paihia, but also make pickups in Russell.

Operated by **Fullers GreatSights** (09/402-7421 or 0800/653-339, www.dolphincruises.co.nz), the Cream Trip departs Paihia daily at 9:30 A.M. and Russell at 9:40 A.M., and cruises leisurely around many of the beautiful islands in the bay, the captain's commentary keeping passengers informed and amused. Following a historic route (it once delivered cream, hence the name), the boat makes short stops at many of the islands to deliver mail and groceries to the farmers and island-caretakers scattered around the bay. The cruise also includes Cape Brett, Motukokako Island, and Cathedral Cave. The cost is adult $109, child $54.50, including a one-hour stop for lunch at picturesque Otehei Bay on Urupukapuka Island. Lunch itself is extra—sandwiches, filled rolls, lamb burgers, snacks, and ice cream are available—or you can bring your own. After lunch there's time for a quick swim or a walk up the hill for good views. Swimming with dolphins is an additional $30.

The most unusual and stylish way to tour the bay is onboard the stunning **R. Tucker Thompson** (09/402-7421 or 0800/653-339, www.dolphincruises.co.nz), a gaff-rigged square topsail schooner that has circumnavigated the world, taken part in Australia's Bicentenary as one of the tall ships reenacting the Australian First Fleet voyage, and starred in the TV series *Adventurer*. Take part in the sailing or just relax; you'll stop at an island (with time for swimming) and savor a barbecue lunch and then afternoon tea. Departing Russell at 10 A.M., the relaxing trip is six to seven hours long. Take a swimsuit, towel, sunblock, warm jacket, and lunch. The cost of the six-hour summer-only trip is adult $145, child $72.50.

Skippered by round-the-world sailor Vanessa McKay, the *Carino* (09/402-8040) is a 50-foot catamaran that departs Paihia on regularly scheduled trips through the Bay of Islands. Go day sailing (eight hours; adult $90, child $50), which includes morning and afternoon tea, fishing and snorkeling gear, swimming with dolphins, sailing lessons, and barbecue lunch on a deserted beach.

For the sailing enthusiast or would-be sailing enthusiast, **Great Escape Yacht Charters** (09/402-7143, www.greatescape.co.nz) provides two- to three-berth yachts complete with outboard auxiliary, stove, and cooking equipment. The cost is from $160 per day, or pay $690 for two days' instruction plus a three-day bareboat charter.

Fishing

The Bay of Islands is New Zealand's most popular game-fishing ground, and fishing is a year-round activity. Some say the best game fishing is in February and March, others claim June and July, but keep in mind that plenty of "big ones" are also caught in January, April, and May. Striped, blue, and black marlin; mako, thresher, blue, and hammerhead sharks; yellowfin tuna; and yellowtail (or kingfish) cruise the waters in abundance. The most prolific big-game fish is the striped marlin; the best months are December–June. For sharks, the best time is November–May, and for tuna, it's December–March. Yellowtail are caught year-round but are mainly fished during June and July. But it's not all big-game fishing fun. Plenty of light-tackle experiences are available from smaller boats.

Paihia Wharf is a hub of deep-sea fishing activity. This town is home base to most of the local game-fishing boats, many of which can be booked through **Pacific Promotions** (09/528-8900, www.fishingpro.co.nz). A solo game-fishing charter starts at $1,200 per day; a share charter (maximum four people) starts at $400 per person. Non-angling passengers can go along to watch the action for considerably less.

The **Bay of Islands Swordfish Club** (09/403-7857, www.swordfish.co.nz) at both the Russell and Paihia waterfronts hosts many of the big-game fishing tournaments. Tournaments are plentiful from Tutukaka to the Bay of Islands from January through June. Club officials perform the weigh-ins and record the vitals whenever a game fish is brought in. You can buy day membership for $15 before going fishing, which includes an official weigh-in and certificate and eligibility for most club trophies. Look for a crowd gathering around either Russell or Paihia wharf, as it's likely to mean they're bringing in a magnificent game fish for a weigh-in. Records of these weigh-ins are written on blackboards by 4 P.M. daily, and displayed at both wharves. There's a good licensed restaurant at the Russell club

Paihia

© ANDREW HEMPSTEAD

NORTHLAND

remote atolls in the South Pacific Ocean. It was later moved north to create an artificial reef; it's now covered in brightly colored marinelife and is a feeding ground for a variety of fish. **Paihia Dive** (Williams Rd., 09/402-7551, www.divenz. com; $399 per person), based in Paihia, offers trips to the wreck. The cost includes the boat ride, all equipment, and two dives.

PAIHIA AND WAITANGI

Paihia (pop. 1,800) is the commercial hub of the Bay of Islands—its streets are lined with tour operators, accommodations, and restaurants. Opposite downtown is **Paihia Wharf,** the departure point for cruises, but also a great place to soak up the Bay of Islands' vacation atmosphere.

From Paihia, continue north along the waterfront to the first intersection and go straight ahead toward Waitangi (if you turn left you'll reach Haruru Falls) and one of New Zealand's most historically important sights.

for members, affiliated and kindred members from an overseas club, and guests of members.

Sea Kayaking

If you've always wanted to try sea kayaking, contact **Island Kayaks** (Marsden Rd., 09/402-6078). This company offers two options: a guided day trip (instruction included) to a local winery for $89, and through a flooded mangrove forest for $75; or you can just rent a single or double sea kayak for $15 per person per hour.

Diving

A diving hot spot was created on December 13, 1987, when the Greenpeace flagship *Rainbow Warrior* settled in 25 meters of water off the Cavalli Islands, south of the entrance to the Bay of Islands. This ship, used by Greenpeace for environmental crusades around the globe, was bombed in 1985 in Auckland Harbour by French intelligence officers trying to prevent Greenpeace from upsetting France's nuclear testing on

◖ Waitangi Treaty Grounds

Waitangi (09/402-7437; daily 9 A.M.–5 P.M.; adult $25, child $12) is the place to absorb New Zealand history and to witness the birthplace of the nation as we know it today. In the Treaty House on February 6, 1840, the Treaty of Waitangi was signed, whereby the Maori surrendered the government of their country to Queen Victoria of Britain in return for protection and "the rights and privileges of British subjects." On first entering this historic park, don't miss the excellent audiovisual show in the Visitor Centre, then stroll through the beautifully kept grounds to the **Treaty House.** Originally designed as a home for British resident James Busby, drafter of the treaty, the house stands in its original condition and is open to the public. Near the Treaty House stands the intricately carved and highly decorated *Whare Runanga* (Maori Meetinghouse), where the local Maori discussed issues, entertained neighboring tribes, and gathered for instruction, storytelling, or

© ANDREW HEMPSTEAD

Treaty House, Waitangi Treaty Grounds

games. The **Maori War Canoe,** on the other side of the reserve, is known to the Maori as *Ngatokimatawhaorua* (The Adzes Which Shaped It Twice) and is adorned with carvings, shells, and feathers. An amazing 35 meters (115 ft) in length, carved from three mighty kauri trees, it has the capacity to carry a crew of 80, plus passengers. If you're planning a visit to this area early in February, check out the annual local celebrations (commemorating the signing of the treaty; the canoe is regularly launched on these occasions.

Even if you're not a history buff, it's worth paying extra (adult $22, child $5, includes general admission) for a one-hour guided tour. Led by a Maori interpreter, these tours go beyond the interpretive panels to bring the grounds and their history to life. Adding further to the experience is the **Waitangi Cultural Performance** (Oct.–Apr. five times daily; adult $5, child $3; purchase with admission ticket), which includes the famous *haka*.

Mount Bledisloe

This mountain marks the northwest boundary of Waitangi Treaty Grounds and is an excellent vantage point. The summit lookout (115 meters/380 ft), a short walk from the parking lot, gives one of the best panoramic views of the Bay of Islands. Follow the road for 3.2 km (two mi) beyond the reserve entrance (passing the rolling fairways of scenic Waitangi Golf Club; 09/402-8207; $60). For an alternate route back to Paihia, turn left on Haruru Falls Road to Haruru Falls, and left again at the main road (Puketona Rd.), which takes you back to Paihia.

Accommodations and Camping

Paihia has one of New Zealand's biggest concentrations of accommodations—over 40 motels and a dozen backpacker lodges within walking distance of the downtown waterfront.

Backpackers are well catered for at Paihia. After undergoing major renovations in 2012, **◖ Peppertree Lodge** (15 Kings Rd.,

09/402-6122, www.peppertree.co.nz, dorm beds $28, $72–110 s or d) is one of the best backpacker lodges. It has a large patio and barbecue area, a lounge and deck, a quiet area stocked with books, a modern kitchen, Internet access, laundry, and bikes and kayaks for use (no charge). Nearby, the popular **Bay Adventurer** (26 Kings Rd., 09/402-5162 or 0800/112-127, www.bayadventurer.co.nz, dorm beds $28, $85–125 s or d) is a purpose-built facility complete with a pool and barbecue area set in a tropical garden, a spa, a lounge equipped with a DVD player, and a large modern kitchen.

Motels in Paihia are among the most expensive in the country, and through January prices are even higher than in "high season." Try the **Dolphin Motel** (69 Williams Rd., 09/402-8170, www.dolphinmotel.co.nz, $145 s, $155 d), where there are 11 self-contained rooms close to the center of town. On the same street is

© ANDREW HEMPSTEAD

Paihia Beach Resort & Spa

Aarangi Tui Motel (16 Williams Rd., 09/402-7496 or 0800/453-354, www.tuimotel.co.nz, from $175 s or d), with one- and two-bedroom units facing a garden area.

Aloha Garden Resort Hotel (36 Seaview Rd., 09/402-7540 or 0800/425-642, www.aloha.co.nz) is set on a two-hectare (five-acre) property complete with a pool and gardens dotted with palm trees. All rooms have cooking facilities, including the smaller studio units with a vaguely nautical theme ($169 s or d) and one-bedroom poolside suites ($189 s or d).

Like Aloha Garden, **Paihia Pacific Resort Hotel** (27 Kings Rd., 09/402-8221, www.paihiapacific.co.nz, $165–220 s or d) is a step above the regular motels in quality, but only a few dollars more. Here, the 35 pastel-themed units open to a courtyard filled with greenery and with a small pool and spa. Other facilities include a restaurant, laundry, and tennis court.

Across the road from the beach, ◖ **Paihia Beach Resort & Spa** (Marsden Rd., 09/402-6140 or 0800/870-111, www.paihiabeach.co.nz) is one of the Bay of Islands' premier accommodations. No expense has been spared in furnishing the luxurious units, each of which has cooking facilities and a large private balcony offering spectacular water views. Raised above street level for extra privacy are a large heated saltwater pool and spa surrounded by stone decking. Rates start at $555 s or d, inclusive of breakfast and one spa treatment.

Adjacent to Waitangi Treaty Grounds, **Copthorne Hotel and Resort** (Tau Henare Dr., 09/402-7411, www.millenniumhotels.com, from $250 s or d) is a sprawling waterfront hotel with all the facilities demanded by the tour-bus crowd, including a restaurant, landscaped pool area, and room service. Check the website for discounted rates that make this place decent value.

Of the several holiday parks in the Paihia area, none are downtown. Winning my vote as the most friendly, **Twin Pines Tourist Park**

(340 Puketona Rd., 09/402-7322, www.twin-pines.co.nz, tents $13 per person, powered sites $15 per person, cabins and self-contained flats $60–100 s or d) is three km (two mi) out along Puketona Road. On the bank of the Waitangi River, adjacent to Haruru Falls (floodlit at night, and heard clearly throughout the campground), the camp has a couple of scenic walks close by (don't miss the steep three-minute bamboo trail from the camp down to the river with its built-in loveseat, view of the falls, and water access).

Beachside Holiday Park (09/402-7678, www.beachsideholiday.co.nz, campsites $18–22 per person, older on-site vans $60 s or d, flats and motel rooms $95–110 s or d) is 2.5 km (1.5 mi) from Paihia, on the road toward Opua and the car ferry to Russell. Set on a private cove, it offers a store, game room, boat ramp and boats for rent, and the usual communal facilities.

© ANDREW HEMPSTEAD

Pahia's Only Seafood restaurant

Food

A string of cafés lines the main road through Paihia, all with water views, outdoor tables, and a beachy atmosphere that makes up for the higher-priced food. Along this stretch, **◖One Hot Tuna** (Marsden Rd., 09/402-5276; daily from 10 A.M.; $9–14) has fantastic fish-and-chips to go.

Among the backpacker lodges on the south side of Paihia, **Beachhouse** (16 Kings Rd., 09/402-7479; daily 8 A.M.–10:30 P.M.; $14–21) has a casual South Pacific vibe, lots of outdoor tables, and occasional evening entertainment. The breakfast menu offers few surprises, but the Tribal Burger, with grilled fish and mango, is delicious.

On the Waitangi Treaty Grounds and surrounded by native forest, **◖ Waikokopu Café** (Te Karuwha Pde., 09/402-6275; daily 9 A.M.–5 P.M.; $11–18) is a world away from touristy Paihia, especially the outdoor tables with filtered ocean views. The charm extends to the menu of casual breakfasts and lunches, which changes seasonally but includes local seafood and usually a Thai-style curry. (I had corn fritters with guacamole, salsa, and sour cream—delicious!)

On the south side of Paihia, **Only Seafood** (40 Marsden Rd., 09/402-6066; daily from 5 P.M.; $28) is a casual seafood restaurant. Downstairs in the same building, **Bistro 40** (09/402-7444; daily from 6 P.M.) goes beyond just seafood and is more upscale.

Practicalities

Information Bay of Islands (Marsden Rd., 09/402-7345, www.visitfarnorth.com; daily 8 A.M.–5 P.M., in summer until 8 P.M.) is beside the Maritime Building. This large facility has boards detailing all cruises and ferry sailings. The post office is on Williams Road, just up from the waterfront.

Scheduled flights between Auckland and the Bay of Islands are operated by **Air New Zealand** (0800/737-000, www.airnewzealand.com) two to four times daily. The airport is

© ANDREW HEMPSTEAD

Peaceful Russell is seemingly a world away from touristy Paihia, just across the bay.

inland from Paihia near Kerikeri (a $38 cab ride from Paihia). **Intercity** (09/623-1503, www.intercity.co.nz) provides bus services between Auckland and Paihia via Whangarei for about $60 one-way. All buses stop outside the Maritime Building.

RUSSELL

Russell (pop. 900) is arguably New Zealand's most picturesque town. Nestled in a west-facing bay and reached by ferry, it lacks the commercialism of Paihia; the streets are lined with historic buildings and elegant cafés and restaurants.

Russell's many historic buildings are all within a couple of blocks of the ferry wharf, but you should start your sightseeing at **Russell Museum** (2 York St., 09/403-7701; daily 10 A.M.–4 P.M.; adult $7.50, child $2). This small museum contains all sorts of relics from early Kororareka (Russell's original name), a fortified Maori settlement, and gives

insight into the people and the history of this colorful town. The highlight and pride of the museum is the seven-meter replica of Captain Cook's ship, the *Endeavour*, accurately reproduced down to the finest detail (Cook and his ship visited Russell in 1769).

Impressive **Pompallier** (The Strand, 09/403-9015; daily 10 A.M.–5 P.M.; adult $5) is a grand old mansion filled with historic relics. Toward the other end of The Strand stands the **police station.** Built in 1870, it has been a customs house, courthouse, and jail, and continues to serve as the Russell police station. Check out the fantastic Morton Bay Fig Tree (*Ficus macrophylla*), with its intricately gnarled and patterned trunk, growing between the police station and the **Duke of Marlborough Hotel.** This old hotel is the proud holder of the first liquor license issued in New Zealand and was among the many "grog shops" of Russell's rowdy past. **Christ Church,** a couple of blocks back from The Strand, was built in 1847 and is the oldest standing church in New Zealand. It still bears cannonball and musket holes from the days of the Maori Wars, and the gravestones (and the stories they tell) in the cemetery are intriguing.

Flagstaff Hill

Also known as Maiki Hill, this historic landmark offers outstanding views of Russell and the Bay of Islands—great for getting oriented and watching all the boats cruising the bay. In the early 1840s, at the top of the hill, the British raised a flagstaff. Hone Heke, chief of the Ngapuhi, saw the flagstaff as a symbol of British authority (for which he had little respect). He and his warriors spent much of their time through the years chopping it down, despite British attempts to keep the flag flying. It wasn't until 1857 that a permanent reconciliation between the Maori and the British formed. At the top of the hill is a monument to these historic events. A two-km/one-mi (30-minute) track up the hill begins at the boat-ramp end of The Strand, follows the beach around to Watering Bay, and then heads up through native bush to the flagstaff. At high tide, take Wellington Street up instead of the track. By car, take Queen Street out of town and follow signs to the top.

Entertainment

There's not a lot of wild nightlife in the Bay of Islands—it's more of a wind-down-and-relax kind of place. Overlooking the beach, the **Duke of Marlborough Hotel** (35 The Strand, 09/403-7829; daily from 11 A.M.) is a favorite watering hole, and has been since 1840 when it was issued New Zealand's very first liquor license. In the main hotel, the **Cane Lounge** is a quiet place with an oceanfront deck and an open fire inside. The adjacent tavern is the most popular locals' spot—the perfect place to enjoy a drink and soak up some of the history that permeates the surroundings.

Accommodations and Camping

Russell Top 10 Holiday Park (Longbeach Rd., 09/403-7826, www.russelltop10.co.nz) offers the least expensive downtown accommodations. It is a well-maintained facility with well-spaced campsites ($36–44), basic cabins ($85–110 s or d), kitchen cabins ($135), and motel rooms ($195). Facilities include a TV room, a kitchen/dining complex, spotless bathrooms (metered showers complete with soft piped music), and a playground.

If you have a vehicle, consider **Wainui Backpackers** (92 Te Wahapu Rd., 09/403-8278, Nov.–Apr., $32), halfway between Russell and the Opua ferry. Surrounded by magnificent bushland, it has just one three-bed dorm and one double room, but all the usual communal facilities are on hand, as well as a dinghy for guest use on the nearby bay.

Behind the waterfront are a few motels, each within easy walking distance of the main wharf but priced higher than almost anywhere else in New Zealand. **Motel Russell** (16 Matauwhi Bay Rd., 09/403-7854, www.motelrussell.co.nz, $145–275 s or d) offers 15 uninspiring motel rooms, each with a kitchen. The one- and two-bedroom units are a good choice for families. The property's selling point is a beautifully landscaped outdoor swimming pool, one of the few in Russell.

Dating from 1899, ◖ **Arcadia Lodge** (10 Florance Ave., 09/403-7756, www.arcadialodge. co.nz, $195–310 s or d includes breakfast) is an elegant accommodation high above the waterfront. Constructed from a great variety of materials collected from around the area, including kauri and wood salvaged from shipwrecks, the lodge is surrounded by extensive gardens. The six guest rooms lie on two levels; each has been elegantly outfitted in stylish furnishings and light pastels. Communal areas include a large lounge, complete with a piano and library.

The **Duke of Marlborough Hotel** (35 The Strand, 09/403-7829, www.theduke.co.nz, $195–360 s or d) has proudly overlooked Russell Harbour since 1840. The 26 rooms are medium-sized and furnished casually, in keeping with the general feel of the place.

Food

The restaurants along Russell's waterfront provide many choices, but you're paying for the delightful location more than anything else. The exception is **The Wharf** (29 The Strand, 09/403-7771; daily for breakfast, lunch, and dinner; $27.50–39), where the most sought-after tables are spread around a grassed area shaded by *pohutukawa* trees and within full view of the setting sun. The menu is filled with classic Pacific Rim dishes, such as prawn and avocado crepes to start and mains like char-grilled game fish with kiwifruit salsa. Stay nationalistic by ordering the kiwifruit pavlova for dessert.

Practicalities

A small information center is on the main wharf (09/403-8020; summer 8:30 A.M.–5 P.M.), or go to the DOC **Russell Visitor Centre** (The Strand, 09/403-9005; summer daily 9 A.M.–5 P.M., the rest of the year Mon.–Fri. 9 A.M.–4:30 P.M.).

Passenger ferries run regularly between Paihia's main wharf and downtown Russell (adult $12, child $6 round-trip). They operate at least once an hour 7 A.M.–7 P.M., with later sailings most nights. The short trip takes just five minutes, and although reservations aren't accepted you can call 09/403-8288 for information. It's also possible to reach Russell by road. From Opua, four km (2.5 mi) south of Paihia, a small vehicular ferry crosses to Okiato, from where it's a pleasant 16-km (10-mi) drive to Russell. The ferry costs $10 per vehicle and driver one-way, plus $1 per passenger. It operates daily 7 A.M.–9 P.M.

If your time in Russell is limited, jump aboard a minibus (they wait by the ferry dock) operated by **Russell Mini Tour** (09/403-7866; departs hourly 10 A.M.–4 P.M.; adult $29, child $14.50) for a one-hour tour of town.

KERIKERI

This historic town (pop. 5,000), 23 km (14 mi) from Paihia, is well worth a visit. Once the home of Chief Hongi Hika and the Ngapuhi warriors, who conquered much of the North Island in the late 18th and early 19th centuries, it was also the site of one of the earliest missions. Kerikeri boasts impressive buildings and trees, lush agricultural land, and the attractive Kerikeri River and Rainbow Falls. It's a citrus center (the signs proclaim it "The Fruitbowl of the North"), quite obvious by the great number of orchards lining the roads between Paihia and Kerikeri, and from the delicious oranges, mandarins, and tangelos available June through January. It's also rapidly becoming an important kiwi cultivating center.

◖ Kerikeri Basin

The historic hub of Kerikeri is this quiet waterway north of downtown, off the main highway along Kerikeri Inlet Road. Overlooking the waterway is New Zealand's oldest European stone building, the **Stone Store** (09/407-9236; summer daily 10 A.M.–5 P.M., the rest of the year daily 10 A.M.–4 P.M.; adult $3.50). Built by the Church Missionary Society in 1832, the Stone Store once served as an impenetrable place of refuge in troubled times and as a storehouse. Still used as a storehouse today, it is under renovation. In recent times it has been used to display articles that belonged to early settlers and knickknacks from the past, and as an outlet for groceries and souvenirs. **Mission House** (same contact and hours as the Stone Store; adult $5, child $3), also known as Kemp House, was built in 1822 and lays claim to being the oldest wooden building in the country. It has been preserved by the Historic Society in much the same state as when the early missionaries lived there, and the surrounding gardens remain beautiful despite the damage caused by severe flooding in 1981. Across the road is a grassy knoll (pleasant spot for a picnic) overlooking Kerikeri Basin. The knoll is the remains of **Kororipo Pa,** a fishing base built by Hongi Hika and other Ngapuhi chiefs, where many historic meetings took place.

Rewa's Village (09/407-6454; summer daily 10 A.M.–5 P.M., the rest of the year daily 10 A.M.–4 P.M.; adult $5, child $2), a reconstruction of a pre-European *kainga* or unfortified Maori village, is a short stroll up the hill facing the Stone Store. To get there, cross the bridge opposite Mission House and look for the parking lot on the left side of the road. On the other side of the road is a trail that winds through the bush and up the hillside to the village. Along the trail many of the native plants are labeled with their names and Maori uses, and at the top you'll find a variety of interesting identified structures and dwellings.

© ANDREW HEMPSTEAD

Stone Store, Kerikeri

Rainbow Falls Scenic Reserve

You can easily reach the top of spectacular Rainbow Falls by road, or the bottom by foot. The water plummets 27 meters (89 ft) over eroded soft lava columns, and there are several viewing points. To get to the falls, enter the reserve off Waipapa Road about two km (1.2 mi) beyond Kerikeri Basin. The road to the falls is well signposted and there's a large parking lot; a 10-minute walk through native bush brings you to the various lookouts. From the second lookout at the top, on a sunny day, you can see how the falls got their name.

Alternatively, a four-km/2.5-mi (one-hour) one-way trail begins across the river from the Stone Store; it follows the Kerikeri River, passes Fairy Pools (good swimming), and comes out at the bottom of the falls. Fairy Pools is also easily reached along a walking trail just south of YHA Kerikeri.

Shopping

Kerikeri distinctly appeals to arts and crafts collectors and music lovers. The town supports a large community of artists; spinning and weaving, ceramics, and stained-glass art are most popular (the shopping center lies off the main road to the right just before Cobham Rd.). Don't miss a stop at **Origin Art & Craft** (128 Kerikeri Rd., 09/407-1133; daily 9:30 A.M.–5 P.M.). Inside you'll discover pottery, knitwear, weaving, stained glass, leatherwork, woodwork, and furniture—it's a shopper's delight—and major credit cards are accepted, just to remove any last doubts you may have about buying up the entire shop.

Accommodations

Kerikeri Farm Hostel (1574 Springbank Rd., 09/407-6989, dorm beds $24, $50 s, $64 d) is set on a seven-hectare (17-acre) orchard five km (three mi) from downtown off Highway 10. It's a small place, but the rooms are comfortable, and guests can use a relaxing lounge area and an outdoor swimming pool.

© ANDREW HEMPSTEAD

Avalon Resort is a peaceful retreat near Kerikeri.

My pick of Kerikeri lodgings, for both value and the delightful setting, is ((**Avalon Resort** (340 Kerikeri Rd., 09/407-1201, www.avalon-resort.co.nz, $150–250 s or d), comprising four cottages and two studio units set on a sprawling property that slopes down to the river (where a kayak is available for guest use). A unique spring-fed swimming pool is surrounded by landscaped palm trees, while ducks and other farm animals scatter themselves around the grounds. The cabins are beautifully decorated with teak furniture and wide balconies, and each has a kitchen.

Kauri Cliffs (Matauri Bay Rd., 09/407-0010, www.kauricliffs.com, from $1,575 s, $1,980 d inclusive of meals) takes on the world's best golf resorts with spacious rooms filled with modern conveniences, an array of spa services and fitness facilities, fine dining, and the pièce de résistance, one of the world's top golf courses, perched high on ocean cliffs and with water views on all but three holes.

Food

Several cafés lie along the main street of Kerikeri, including **Kerikeri Bakehouse** (334 Kerikeri Rd., 09/407-7266; daily 7 A.M.–4 P.M.; $10–16) for fully cooked breakfasts and lunch choices such as steak sandwiches and antipasto platters. Overlooking Kerikeri Basin, **Pear Tree** (215 Kerikeri Rd., 09/407-8479; daily 10 A.M.–9 P.M.; $19–31) has a sunny outlook and a wide-ranging menu that covers all bases. Dinner mains include seared venison and fish poached in saffron sauce

BAY OF ISLANDS TO KAITAIA

The most direct route between the Bay of Islands and Kaitaia, gateway to Cape Reinga, is to backtrack from Paihia the short distance to Highway 1, which cuts across Northland via Mangamuka Bridge.

The following section details the longer alternative, Highway 10, giving the traveler-in-a-hurry the opportunity to absorb beautiful coastal scenery while driving, yet luring the hiker and nature enthusiast into frequent stops to smell the flowers. Scenic reserves intermingled with fir tree plantations line the highway, soft white-sand beaches lead you to the ocean, and in summer wildflowers border the roads. In some areas, endless rows of pine trees follow the contours of the land—planted as a windbreak, these magnificent hedges separate the rolling hills and fields into giant patchworks of color.

Whangaroa

The several small towns along Highway 10 share a relaxed atmosphere. Fishing boats, small private beaches, cottage arts and crafts, and tempting tearooms may delay your venture north. Like being on the water? Take a sidetrack to Whangaroa, six km (3.7 mi) north of **Kaeo.** Beautiful Whangaroa Harbour has become a renowned spot for excellent fishing—some say it's much better than the Bay of Islands. Charter boats are always available,

NORTHLAND

and in recent years local boats have captured a large number of blue, black, and striped marlin.

On the shores of Whangaroa Harbour, **Sunseeker Lodge** (Old Hospital Rd., 09/405-0496, www.sunseekerlodge.co.nz, dorm beds $30, $120–150 s or d) is known for its friendly atmosphere and magnificent harbor views from its elevated location. It's the kind of place where you plan to stay a night but end up staying a week. A dinghy and fishing gear can be rented, and big-game fishing trips and harbor cruises can be arranged. Sea kayaks are also available.

Continuing north from Whangaroa Harbour, **Kahoe Farms Hostel** (Hwy. 10, 10 km/six mi north of Kaeo, 09/405-1804, www.kahoefarms.co.nz, dorm beds $27, $54 s, $70–90 d) is in a beautiful setting, and it's a good base from which to explore this area of Northland. Take a short walk from the farmhouse and up a small hill on the property for great views across Whangaroa Harbour. The hosts arrange a variety of local activities, including trips to Cape Reinga.

Mangonui

The picturesque village of Mangonui, 30 km (19 mi) northwest of Whangaroa, lies on the southern edge of **Doubtless Bay,** marked as being "doubtless a bay" when Captain Cook sailed by in the late 1700s. Mangonui was originally a busy whaling base and trading station. In recent years, although the main undertaking is commercial fishing, southerners have discovered the charm of the area and the population has rapidly increased.

Ask a local for directions to the top of **Rangikapiti Pa.** The brilliant 360-degree view brings the whole area into perspective, and you can walk or drive to the top. Boats can be rented for fishing (from $20 an hour with an outboard)—though you can catch snapper, John Dory, and kingfish from the wharf on an incoming tide.

If you're looking for somewhere to stay,

make reservations at **The Old Oak** (66 Waterfront Dr., 09/406-1250, www.theoldoak.co.nz, $125 s, $175–295 d). You can't miss it—made of pit-sawn kauri and established in 1861, the two-story white-washed hotel stands directly across from the Mangonui waterfront. The seven guest rooms, which underwent serious renovations in 2009, have an air of casual elegance, with super-comfortable beds and well-equipped bathrooms. Downstairs, the **Acorn Bar & Bistro** (breakfast, lunch, and dinner in summer; $26–31) will lure you in for a delicious continental breakfast ($17.50) and then back again in the evening for a short but delicious menu of creative New Zealand fare. Continue along the road to the **Waterfront Cafe** (Waterfront Dr., 09/406-0850; daily from 8 A.M.; $15–24), a local favorite for seafood chowder, smoked fish pie (using fresh fish from local waters), huge addictive bacon rolls, pizzas, cappuccino, and freshly brewed coffee.

Doubtless Bay to Kaitaia

West of Mangonui, Highway 10 hugs the southern shore of Doubtless Bay, passing **Coopers Beach, Cable Bay,** and **Taipa,** all known for their white-sand beaches and handsome groves of *pohutukawa* trees. Coopers Beach has a campground and motor camp. Though Cable Bay's small beach is attractive to campers, it's a reserve, so camping is not permitted. After crossing the Taipa River you enter the town of Taipa, with another fairly large motor camp. You can get great views of the Tokerau Beach peninsula and Cape Karikari from the Taipa area. Accessible on an unpaved road (turn off Hwy. 10 west of Taipa), the remote **Karikari Peninsula** offers more beaches and delightful coves, including **Matai Bay.**

After leaving Doubtless Bay, Highway 10 crosses a rolling rural landscape to Awanui and Kaitaia, 50 km (31 mi) from Taipa.

Kaitaia to Cape Reinga

Gateway to New Zealand's northern tip is the town of Kaitaia, 110 km (68 mi) from Paihia and 330 km (205 mi) from Auckland. From Awanui, eight km (five mi) north of Kaitaia at the junction of Highways 1 and 10, it's just over 100 km (62 mi) along the spine of the Aupouri Peninsula to Cape Reinga, with the last 21 km (13 km), from Waitiki Landing, unsealed. The alternative to the road is driving along Ninety Mile Beach, along the west side of the peninsula. The beach is not recommended for regular vehicles, but this is the route taken by bus tours—either on the outward or return trip.

KAITAIA

This bustling town (pop. 5,400) is the gateway to the far north, but also has an interesting museum and is near the ruggedly scenic beachside town of Ahipara.

The excellent **Far North Museum** (6 South Rd., 09/408-1403; weekdays 10 A.M.–5 P.M.; $5 adult, $2 child) is a trove of information on the historical aspects of the northern region. Displays focus on ancient Maori lifestyles, including agricultural, fishing, and hunting methods and equipment, intricate feather capes and articles of clothing, and a comprehensive display of Maori carving styles and art forms. Other highlights include a display of New Zealand birds, an ancient anchor and various shipwreck articles, and a 1909–1936 photograph collection featuring kauri-gum-digging activities. Don't miss the information board at the entrance, where descriptions and prices of all the latest tours up the cape are advertised.

Accommodations

In the heart of town, **Mainstreet Lodge** (235 Commerce St., 09/408-1275, www.mainstreetlodge.co.nz) is a popular budget accommodation where hospitable owners arrange tours

throughout the Far North and throw the occasional *hangi* (Maori feast). Facilities include powerful hot showers, two modern kitchens, an outdoor barbecue area and pizza oven, a sunny dining room, a lounge, Internet access, laundry, and bicycles. Options include dorm beds ($27–31) or private rooms ($58–68 s, $64–72 d).

Kauri Lodge Motel (15 South Rd., 09/408-1190, www.kaurilodgemotel.co.nz, $89–115 s or d) is handily located directly opposite the information center. Each of the eight guest rooms has a kitchen, and there's a small outdoor swimming pool for guest use.

Food

Dining at the **Bushman's Hut** (corner of Bank St. and Puckey Ave., 09/408-4320; Wed.–Fri. for lunch, daily from 6 P.M. for dinner; $17–29) is more expensive than at the pubs around town, but the atmosphere is a little more sophisticated (it's all relative in small-town New Zealand) and the steaks are cooked exactly to order. **Beachcomber** (222 Commerce St., 09/408-2010; Mon.–Sat. 11 A.M.–2:30 P.M. and 5–8:30 P.M., $16–30) serves seafood, steak, and chicken. The food is better than the decor may suggest.

Information and Services

Far North Information Centre (South Rd., 09/408-0879, www.visitfarnorthnz.com, summer daily 8:30 A.M.–5 P.M., the rest of the year Mon.–Fri. 8:30 A.M.–5 P.M.) is by Jaycee Park at the southern entrance to town.

The main street downtown is Commerce Street, on which you'll find the post office (104 Commerce St.), **Bank of New Zealand** (with ATM, 108 Commerce St.), Internet access at **Vodaphone** (84 Commerce St.), and a coin laundry (Kaitaia Plaza). **Kaitaia Hospital** (09/408-0010) and the police station (09/408-6500) are both on Redan Road, off Commerce Street heading toward Ahipara.

Getting There

Kaitaia Airport, nine km (six mi) north of town, is served by **Air New Zealand** (0800/737-000, www.airnewzealand.com) from Auckland. Cabs await all arrivals.

Kaitaia is the northernmost stop on the **Intercity** (www.intercity.co.nz) bus network. From the depot at **Far North Information Centre** (South Rd., 09/408-0879), buses arrive and depart once daily for all points south, via Paihia and Whangarei.

AHIPARA

Spread around Ahipara Bay, 15 km (nine mi) southwest of Kaitaia and at the southern end of Ninety Mile Beach, this is a popular place for New Zealanders with four-wheel drives and those who enjoy beach fishing.

Just above Ahipara is **Gumdiggers Park** (171 Heath Rd., 09/406-7166; daily 9 A.M.–5 P.M.; adult $12, child $6), a stark, barren plateau that was home to hundreds of Yugoslav gum diggers in the 1890s. Vast forests of kauri trees once covered the north, but most of these forests were quickly decimated by the colonial timber-cutters of the early 1800s. Over many centuries, kauri resin, which hardens into gum on contact with air, had dribbled down the trees, collected around the bases, and petrified under forest debris. When the timber rush finished, the gum rush began. The ground where mighty trees once stood was dug up, denuded of its gum, and made barren. By the 1890s the fossilized gum, used as a base for slow-drying hard varnishes and for making linoleum, had become one of New Zealand's major exports. Most of the gum fields of the north have been ploughed and fertilized into agricultural land, but the Ahipara Plateau has been preserved as a reminder of the past.

Accommodations and Camping

Ahipara Bay Motel (22 Reef View Rd., 09/409-4888 or 0800/909-453; from $115 s or

d) is a modern motel complex overlooking the ocean. Rooms have kitchens, and a couple of smaller studio units offer fantastic views. The property has a restaurant and bar, and guests can rent beach-fishing gear.

Views from the ◖ **Siesta Lodge** (Tasman Heights Rd., 09/409-4565, www.siesta.co.nz, $250 s or d includes breakfast) and its surrounding garden are stunning—a 180-degree panorama of the south end of Ninety Mile Beach—and the beach is only a few hundred meters away. The house has a guest wing, where the rooms feature timbered ceilings, comfortable beds, private bathrooms, writing desks, and balconies with views.

It's just a five-minute walk to the beach from **Ahipara Holiday Park** (Takahe St., 09/407-4864, www.ahiparaholidaypark.co.nz, campsites $15–17, cabins $65–95 s or d, motel rooms $125). Communal facilities, indoor dining, a swimming pool, and a barbecue round out the features.

KAITAIA TO THE CAPE: THE INLAND ROUTE

Most travelers who reach Kaitaia have one destination in mind—Cape Reinga. From the turnoff at Awanui, eight km (five mi) north of Kaitaia, it's 104 km (64 mi) up the Aupouri Peninsula to the cape. Traveling north, the landscape progressively gets drier. The colorful fields become scrubland, and exotic pine plantations are the only evidence of human changes to this desert-like landscape. Huge sand dunes roll in all directions, and the large saltwater marshes brim with birdlife. In March, on the mighty dunes of the north, the *kuakas* or Eastern bar-tailed godwits gather in great numbers before their annual migration to breeding grounds on the Alaskan and Siberian tundra. Much of the peninsula has been made into a reserve, thus protecting it from development and other intrusion.

Waipapakauri Beach, 18 km (11 mi) north of Kaitaia and the southern access point for tours along Ninety Mile Beach, is home to **Ninety Mile Beach Holiday Park** (6 Matai St., 09/407-7298 or 0800/367-719, www.ninetymilebeach. co.nz, campsites $16 per person, cabins $75–105 s or d), a large and popular commercial campground. Bathroom, kitchen, and laundry facilities are communal; there's also a game room with Internet access, barbecues, a café, and general store.

Houhora Harbour and Beyond

This long, narrow body of water 40 km (25 mi) north of Kaitaia makes a good stopping point on the trip to the cape. Turn east onto Houhora Heads Road to reach **Houhora Heads,** at the entrance to the harbor. Here, **Houhora Chalets Motor Lodge** (Houhora Heads Rd., 09/409-8860, $80–100 s or d) offers six self-contained rooms and a swimming pool.

Continuing north, **Pukenui Lodge Motel** (Wharf Rd., 09/409-8837, www.pukenuilodge. co.nz, dorm beds $27, $70 s or d, motel rooms $125 s or d) is on the main highway north in Pukenui, overlooking Houhora Harbour. Facilities include a game room, pool, and barbecue in landscaped grounds. Explore the beaches or go diving or fishing; you can rent a dinghy or mountain bikes at the motel, and across the road are a restaurant and café.

From Pukenui, it's 68 km (42 mi) to Cape Reinga. Take the side road west from Te Kao to **The Bluff,** an excellent area to view Ninety Mile Beach in both directions; the surf is good, and the hard, white sand is covered with shells. Offshore lies Wakatehaua Island.

The last services are at **Waitiki Landing Complex** (09/409-7508), 21 km (13 mi) from the cape, offering groceries, fuel, a laundry, and a restaurant. Camping is $22, dorm beds are $26, and simple cabins $80 s or d.

█ NINETY MILE BEACH

Abel Tasman called these northwestern shores "the desert coast." The etymology of "Ninety Mile Beach" remains unknown, although you could easily be forgiven for estimating this unbroken stretch of sand at 90 miles. The beach is actually 56 miles in length, or almost exactly 90 km—the name-giver must have been an early advocate of the metric system. Huge white sand dunes reaching 143 meters (470 ft) high and six km (3.7 mi) wide fringe the beach, kept in place by mass plantings of marram grass and pine trees.

Every January, reels scream and large game-fish dance in the shallows off Ninety Mile Beach as hordes of anglers compete for big-money prizes in one of the world's largest surf-fishing contests. Apart from being a shell-collector's paradise, this amazing beach is well known for good surfing conditions, particularly at Ahipara and Wreck Bay (walk around the rocks from the Ahipara access). All beach users should beware: Every now and again an unexpected roller will come way up the beach or rocks, submerging previously safe areas; keep way back from the water's edge.

Driving Ninety Mile Beach

The sand below the high-water mark along Ninety Mile Beach is concrete-hard, at times solid enough to support motor vehicles. During low spring tides, a belt of about 250 meters (820 ft) of sand is considered safe under normal conditions for motoring. The main access point is the village of Waipapakauri Beach in the south and the northern pull-off point is the Bluff. Experienced 4WD enthusiasts often continue to Te Paki stream. The Automobile Association recommends that you not drive on it for at least three hours before and after high tide. The sand is safe to *drive* on, but don't leave the car standing on wet sand for even a short time: the wheels can sink very rapidly. All rental car firms specify no driving on Ninety Mile Beach. The safest way to enjoy the unique opportunity of driving along the beach is on an organized Cape Reinga bus tour.

JOURNEY OF THE DEAD

The main legend of Northland concerns the final trip of ancient Maori spirits of the dead. The legend says that after death, the Maori spirits padded up Te-Oneroa-A-Tohe (the Maori version of Ninety Mile Beach, not a direct translation) with a token of home in hand. The spirits left the token at Te Arai Bluff, then continued to Scott Point, where they climbed the highest hill and took a last look back at the land of the living. After quenching their thirst in Re-Wai-O-Raio-Po, the stream of the underworld, they trudged on to Cape Reinga. At the northern tip of this rocky promontory you can see the famed *pohutukawa* tree with its exposed root, which the spirits slid down before gently dropping into the sea. The kelp parted, and they swam to the Three Kings Island. After surfacing for a last look at New Zealand, the spirits took up the trail to Hawaiiki, their Polynesian homeland. Legend also states that the spirits of the sick sometimes got as far as Te-Oneroa-A-Tohe, but if they didn't quench their thirst at the stream, the spirits returned to their bodies.

CAPE REINGA

The road up Aupouri Peninsula ends at an elevated parking lot 108 km (67 mi) north of Kaitaia. From this exposed promontory you get tremendous views in all directions. Looking eastward you can see **North Cape** and the **Surville Cliffs.** To the west lies **Cape Maria Van Diemen,** and on the northern horizon, 57 km (35 mi) off Cape Reinga, are the **Three Kings Islands.** This nature reserve, made up of 40 islands and rocks, is clearly visible from the cape only in fine weather. Also to the north and not far offshore is **Columbia Bank,** the point at which the Tasman Sea and the Pacific Ocean converge. Look for turbulent water and large crashing waves—in stormy weather they can reach up to 10 meters (33 ft) high. If you walk to the very tip of the cape, you'll see the famed *pohutukawa* tree, the roots of which are the legendary path for Maori spirits of the dead. Cape Reinga has no facilities, just the well-known whitewashed **Cape Reinga Lighthouse.**

Walking

The northern section of the New Zealand Walkway starts at Cape Reinga. Don't attempt any of the tracks without a map, and come adequately prepared for beach camping—there are no overnight huts. If you plan to hike all the tracks, start at the eastern end of Spirits Bay. A 28-km (17-mi) track runs from Spirits Bay to Cape Reinga, involves some steep sections toward the end, and takes about 10 hours. From Cape Reinga a 22-km (14-mi) cliff-and-beach track heads south to Te Paki Stream (look out for treacherous quicksand in this area), taking about seven hours. The next track starts at Te Paki Stream and follows Ninety Mile Beach all the way down to Ahipara, at the south end of the beach. It takes a good two to three days to hike the entire 83 km (52 mi) to Ahipara, but you can leave the track and get back onto the main road at the Bluff (19 km/12 mi), Hukatere (51 km/32 mi), or Waipapakauri (69 km/43 mi). Many other walking tracks in Te Paki Farm Park lead to points of historical or archeological interest and scenic lookouts—pick and choose from a short 30-minute walk to a several-day hike.

Expect to cover beaches, sand dunes, swamps, and pastureland during the various hikes, and be sure to take plenty of water, energy food, sunscreen, and insect repellent. A large map with lengths, times, and descriptions of the various tracks is posted in Cape Reinga's parking area. For more information and maps, see the ranger at Waitiki Landing (on the main road to the cape) or call in at the Information

CAPE REINGA TOURS

Driving to the end of the road is only half of the Cape Reinga experience. Take one of the many guided tours, and make the return (or vice versa, depending on the tides) journey along the hard-packed sands of **Ninety Mile Beach**. From Kaitaia, **Sand Safaris** (221 Commerce St., 09/408-1778 or 0800/869-090, www.sandsafaris.co.nz) departs daily at 9 A.M. for the cape. The tour travels along the beach in one direction, while also taking in the Te Paki Sand Dunes, Cape Reinga, east coast beaches, and Aupouri Forest. You can also try sand surfing. The cost of adult $50, child $30 includes lunch and accommodation pickups in Kaitaia. Departing from Kaitaia as well is the highly recommended **Far North Outback Adventures** (09/408-0927, www.farnorthtours.co.nz). The cost is a little higher than the other options, but the tour is a lot more personalized and the knowledge of guide Phil Cross is priceless.

Tours also leave from Paihia, in the Bay of Islands. **Fullers GreatSights** (0800/653-339, www.dolphincruises.co.nz) departs Paihia daily at 7:15 A.M., including all of the Sand Safaris stops in one long day tour; adult $129, child $64.50, optional lunch $23.

Centre on South Road in Kaitaia. For fairly detailed maps and track descriptions, pick up the free booklet *New Zealand Walkway—Walks in the Northland District* or the *New Zealand Walkway—Far North* brochure.

Camping

The closest accommodation to the cape is **Waitiki Landing Complex** (09/409-7508, camping $22, dorm beds $26, cabins $80), 21 km (13 mi) to the south. If you don't mind roughing it for a night or two, you can camp at a couple of places farther north. Most have fresh water and some have toilets, but some have no facilities at all. Try the campground at **Tapotupotu Bay** (45 sites, $7 per person). Three km (1.9 mi) from the main road and signposted, it's down the northernmost road to the east before Cape Reinga. The campground lies at the back of a beautiful surf beach, and a park ranger supervises it during peak holiday periods from one of the resident caravans. Open all year, it operates on an honesty-box system when the ranger isn't there. The camp has water, toilets, and showers. A stream (considerably warmer than the ocean) runs by the campground and out to sea, and the beach, pounded by big surf, is a long stretch of golden sand with rock formations at the south end. The campground at **Spirits Bay** ($7 per person), a sacred Maori area, has water, toilets, and showers. Take Te Hapua Road, then Spirits Bay Road to Hooper Point. The campground is a long way from the main road but very handy for hikers doing the Spirits Bay to Cape Reinga Track.

NORTHLAND

Kaitaia to Auckland via the West Coast

From Kaitaia, it's 320 km (200 mi) back down Highway 1 to Auckland. The route followed below detours from Highway 1 47 km (29 mi) south of Kaitaia along the Mangamuka Road and then veers south to Hokianga Harbour, where a short ferry trip will deliver you to a remote region of Northland abutting the Tasman Sea.

SOUTH TO HOKIANGA HARBOUR
Mangamuka Gorge and Walkway

Mangamuka Gorge is a gorgeous drive, particularly on a sunny day, when you'll probably find yourself leaping in and out of the car at regular intervals, camera in hand, to capture giant tree ferns and assorted flora and fauna. Allow plenty of time to meander through all this lushness. Mangamuka Gorge Walkway starts 26 km (16 mi) southeast of Kaitaia and crosses a part of the Maungataniwha Range. The route winds through the beautiful Raetea Forest and Mangamuka Gorge Scenic Reserve, emerging at Highway 1 north of Mangamuka Township. During the hike expect to traverse open farmland, dense forest, and lush native bush with its wonderland of ferns, mosses, and lichens. Climb to the radio mast atop Raetea summit (751 meters/2,494 ft) for spectacular panoramic views of North Cape and Karikari Peninsula to the north, Hokianga Harbour to the south, Bay of Islands to the east, and Tauroa Point and Ahipara to the west. At the summit, the main track doubles back and continues east—don't head south along the minor track toward Broadwood unless it's familiar; this track fizzles out in places and it's easy to get lost in the dense bush. Keep on the main marked track at all times.

The 19-km/12-mi (six- to seven-hour) one-way trail is steep, muddy, and hard going. It's recommended for experienced hikers only, and it's best to have transportation awaiting you at the end. Wear sturdy hiking boots, and carry raingear, a change of warm clothes (the weather can turn bad quickly), food, and water—there are no streams along the ridge. To get to the western entrance, take Highway 1 south of Pamapuria, turn west onto Takahue Valley Road, then turn left on Takahue Saddle Road.

Kaikohe

Highway 1 beyond Mangamuka Gorge runs south to Ohaeawai, where Highway 12 branches west to Kaikohe (pop. 3,500). The countryside around Kaikohe is scattered with historic buildings, and if you're traveling through the town, the local attraction is **Heritage Kaikohe** (Recreation Rd., 09/401-0816; summer Mon.–Sat. 10 A.M.–4 P.M., Sun. 1–4 P.M., the rest of the year Sat. 10 A.M.–4 P.M., Sun. 1–4 P.M.; adult $10, child $2). A re-creation of a 19th-century Northland community, the five-acre grounds contain an indoor and outdoor museum, a bush railway, the original 1864 Waimate North Courthouse building, a kauri gum collection, Maori and pioneer artifacts, a begonia garden, and a narrow-gauge railway.

A good option for an overnight stay is the **New Haven Motel** (36 Raihara St., 09/401-1859, www.newhavenmotel.co.nz, $75–95 s, $85–105 d), just off the main road through town. Each of the 11 guest rooms has tea- and coffee-making facilities and a small fridge; some have small kitchens.

HOKIANGA HARBOUR

Stretching inland for more than 50 km (31 mi), Hokianga Harbour has forged a deep channel almost halfway across Northland to the Bay of Islands. In the early 19th century, this fiordlike harbor was lined with kauri forests and bustling with marine activity. Droves of ships sailed over from Sydney, defying the treacherous sandbars and large surf at the harbor mouth to keep up with demand for kauri timber. Once the shores had been stripped of their slow-growing forests, the timber mills closed and the ships left. Nowadays the harbor lies relatively undisturbed, slowly reverting to its original wildness and desolation. Few roads lead to the tangled mangrove forests, mighty sand dunes, and green valleys that line its shores. The peaceful beauty and quiet attracts quite a community of artists and people into alternative lifestyles; watch for out-of-the-ordinary houses, and for roadside arts-and-crafts stands where you can often pick up real bargains.

The best way to appreciate the harbor is by boat, and you'll find willing operators in Rawene, Opononi, and Omapere. Highway 1 detours east around this mighty harbor toward Okaihau, and the Highway 12 junction to Kaikohe. The shorter and more scenic route is to cross the harbor at the Narrows via car ferry and continue south down Highway 12. To get to the ferry, pass through Mangamuka Scenic Reserve, turn right at Mangamuka Bridge, and go through Kohukohu and on to the Narrows.

Kohukohu and Vicinity

For a shortcut from the north, turn south off Highway 1 at Mangamuka Bridge, then head south on Mohuiti Narrows Road to Kohukohu, a small village with many historic buildings scattered throughout town. Continuing south, the Hokianga Vehicular Ferry is four km (two mi) beyond Kohukohu, or follow the signs two km (one mi) past the ferry landing to the ◖ Tree House (168 West Coast Rd., 09/405-5855, www.treehouse.co.nz, campsites $18 per person, dorm beds $32, cabins $69 s, $82 d), comprising a main building (with lots of stained-glass windows) built by the owners, along with inexpensive cabins. The atmosphere is super-relaxing and there's plenty to do around the surrounding farm and the harbor.

Hokianga Ferry

The *Kohu-Ra* operates daily between the Narrows and Rawene. In summer it departs the Narrows once an hour (usually on the hour) 7:15 A.M.–7:30 P.M., and Rawene every hour 7 A.M.–8 P.M. (fewer sailings in winter). Try to time it so you arrive about 10 to 15 minutes before the crossing—there's nothing to do while you wait (and no facilities), but you need to get in line. The crossing takes about 15 minutes and costs $16 per vehicle and driver plus $4 per passenger each way.

Rawene

Getting off the ferry at Rawene, the third-oldest settlement in New Zealand (pop. 500), feels like taking a step back in time. On your way through, don't miss **Clendon House** on the foreshore (09/405-7874; Nov.–Apr. Sat.–Mon. 10 A.M.–4 P.M.; adult $5, child $2.50). A historic building preserved by the Historic Places Trust, it was built in the late 1860s by James Clendon, ship owner, trader, and the first U.S. consul in New Zealand. The house contains many of the owner's possessions and period furnishings. The **Masonic Hotel** (09/405-7822), built in 1875, is Rawene's local watering hole. You'll also find a small supermarket, a smattering of shops, takeaways, a gas station, and a post office.

Opononi and Omapere

After leaving Rawene, Highway 12 runs east to Kaikohe and Ohaeawai (where it rejoins Hwy. 1), or west to Opononi and Omapere before heading south through the kauri forests.

Situated at the mouth of Hokianga Harbour, the twin towns of Opononi and Omapere (three km apart) boast golden beaches and beautiful views up the harbor and out to sea. At Omapere you can appreciate the harbor best by cruise boat—get the details at the information center. For the best views, turn off Highway 12 just south of Omapere and take the road out to South Head. Opononi became quite well

THE KAURI FORESTS

The forests of Northland provide the nature lover with a wide range of native plant- and birdlife and the chance to appreciate many tree varieties. These include *rimu, rata, towai, kahikatea,* and *tawa,* though all are dwarfed by the magnificent kauri. The kauri (*Agathis australis*) is a conifer, grouped botanically with pines and firs that grow north of latitude 38 degrees south. It is New Zealand's native giant—similar but less majestic trees of the same family can be found in Australia, Malaysia, the Philippines, Fiji, and other Pacific islands. The kauri is easily recognized by its tall columnar trunk (it self-sheds the lower branches), massive heavily branched crown, and thick, leathery leaves. The highly decorative bark is silvery gray and covered in irregular circular patterns. Another characteristic of the older kauri trees is the large mound of *pukahu,* or humus, at the base of the trunk. This mound is made up of bark, shed over several hundred years, and root systems. Note that the kauri is dependent on its surface root network for essential nutrients, and survival depends to a large degree on not having its vital roots trampled—keep on the tracks to ensure these magnificent trees' future.

Some of the trees have been estimated at well over a thousand years old. Their rate of growth is very slow, taking 80 to 100 years to reach millable size. A young kauri is called a "ricker." The timber is straight grained, easily worked, durable, and very popular with carpenters and craftspeople. In the early 1800s, the kauri dominated forest vegetation and covered about three million hectares (7.4 million acres) from the North Cape to Waikato. By the end of the century only one-quarter of the kauri forests remained; the trees had been cut down for shipbuilding, leached for gum, or burned when the land was cleared for agriculture.

Nowadays the policy is to preserve these ancient forests. **Waipoua Forest** and **Trounson Kauri Park,** both on Highway 12 between Hokianga Harbour and Dargaville, provide excellent examples of what all this land looked like before the arrival of Europeans.

---

known in the summer of 1955 when a friendly dolphin the locals named "Opo" came to play with swimmers every day—a memorial statue to the dolphin stands on the oceanfront.

Okopako Lodge (140 Mountain Rd., signposted from Hwy. 12, 09/405-8815, www.yha.co.nz, dorm beds $30, $46 s, $66 d) is part of a working farm. It lacks modern conveniences, but the lodge has a pleasant setting and stunning harbor views. Another budget choice, **Globe Trekkers Lodge** (Hwy. 12, Omapere, 09/405-8183, dorm $31, $51 s, $66 d), is a modern facility with harbor views from a large deck.

Beside the BP service station in Omapere, the **Harbourside Café** (09/405-8238; daily for breakfast and lunch; $7–12) serves a cooked breakfast ($12), pizza slices ($4), and burgers ($7). It's probably one of the few cafés in the country without a deep fryer.

For the rundown on the area, stop at the **Hokianga Information Centre** (09/405-8869; summer daily 8:30 A.M.–5:30 P.M., the rest of the year daily 8:30 A.M.–5 P.M.), on the main road between the two towns. You can also access the Internet from here.

KAURI COAST

Most of the splendid kauri forests along Northland's west coast were logged in the 1800s, but the remaining stands and some wild west coast scenery make the journey between Hokianga Harbour and Dargaville the preferred, albeit longer, alternative to Highway 1.

◖ Waipoua Forest

Beginning about 35 km (22 mi) south of Opononi, Highway 12 runs 16 km (10 mi) through the cool, lush greenery of Waipoua Forest, a place where time seems to stand still. Protected as a sanctuary since the 1950s, this remnant of New Zealand's once-extensive kauri forests covers an area of more than 9,000 hectares (22,240 acres) and contains five known giant trees, each estimated to be at least 1,000 years old. Apart from these giants there are 300 other species of trees, palms, ferns, and mosses, and although it's possible to enjoy the forest from the road, the best way to appreciate the grandeur is to get on some of the tracks. The forest is crisscrossed with trails; great picnic spots abound. The well-marked tracks vary from short 10-minute walks leading to particular kauri giants to longer hikes that offer a far richer assortment of sights and sounds of the forest.

From the north, the first worthwhile stop is for a short hike to 1,200-year-old *Tane Mahuta* (Lord of the Forest). Standing nearly 52 meters (171 ft) high and with a girth of 13 meters (43 ft), it's believed to be the largest kauri in the country.

Continuing south, a 700-meter (2,297-ft) trail leads through a particularly beautiful stretch of forest to *Te Matua Ngahere* (Father of the Forest). Although not as tall as *Tane Mahuta,* this kauri is renowned for its impressive five-meter-wide (16-ft-wide) diameter. Its exact age is unknown, but it may be nearly 2,000 years old. If you have the time, sit opposite the tree for a while and soak up the surroundings. The tranquil beauty of the bush and splendor of the "Father," cheerful birdsong, and buzzing cicadas create a natural high. Nearby is the **Four Sisters,** a group of kauri nestled close together.

The DOC-operated **Waipoua Visitor Centre** (09/439-3011; daily 8:30 A.M.–4 P.M., until 5 P.M. in summer) is off Highway 12 in the southern section of the forest, to the west after crossing Waipoua River (southbound). Stop by for information on forest management, local legends, and walking tracks, and to see the cottage museum, where the lifestyle of a kauri bushman is on display.

Trounson Kauri Park

This small but superb stand of kauri north off

Highway 12 was deeded to the government for protection over 100 years ago. The park now totals 570 hectares (1,409 acres), and a resolute effort has been made to eradicate nonnative species such as rats, possums, and cats. This, in turn, has dramatically increased the park's kiwi population. A walking trail through the heart of the park takes about a half hour round-trip, and the highlight is the Four Sisters tree—actually two kauri trees, each with twin trunks that have grown together as one. At one point the track runs under a fallen kauri for a close-up view, and farther along you can appreciate the root system of a large 600-year-old fallen kauri from a viewing platform.

To see the park's most precious residents, join the owners of nearby **Kauri Coast Top 10 Holiday Park** (09/439-0621 or 0800/807-200) on their hour-long guided evening walk (adult $25, child $15). In addition to kiwis, giant *wekas* and kauri snails are often sighted.

Holiday Park

Accommodations are well spaced along this remote stretch of coastline, but there is one excellent option within the forest, █ **Kauri Coast Top 10 Holiday Park** (09/439-0621 or 0800/807-200, www.kauricoasttop10.co.nz, campsites $25 s, $40 d, cabins $75–120 s or d, motel rooms $135), three km (two mi) along the road to Trounson Kauri Park beside a river dotted with swimming holes and filled with enough rainbow and brown trout to keep any angler happy. A fully equipped kitchen, three barbecue areas, a laundry, and a playground are on-site. The owners also operate a popular evening walk up the road in Trounson Kauri Park (adult $25, child $15).

Kai-Iwi Lakes

South from the kauri forests, turn west (toward the coast) at Maropiu on Omamari Road to access Kai-Iwi Lakes, the collective name for three brilliantly blue freshwater lakes (Kai-Iwi,

Taharoa, and Waikere), great for swimming, fishing, sailing, and water-skiing. In addition, soft white-sand beaches, sheltered bays for swimming and snorkeling, rolling farmland, and lots of pine trees make this an even more attractive place. Lake Taharoa is stocked with trout and offers shoreside camping; on the banks of Lake Waikere is a water-ski club, a hive of activity on summer weekends. Two walks, to **Sandy Bay** (3 km/2 mi; one hour) and to **Maunganui Bluff** (1.8 km/1.1 mi), start on Kai-Iwi Lakes Road.

Dargaville

At the northern end of Wairoa River, Dargaville (pop. 4,500) was originally a busy kauri timber and gum-trading port. When the logging industry went into decline, so did Dargaville, and today it's the small commercial center for the surrounding dairy districts. The hilltop **Dargaville Museum** (Harding Park, 09/439-7555; daily 9 A.M.–5 P.M.; adult $12, senior $10, child $2) displays items of local seafaring interest, the masts from Greenpeace's sunken flagship the *Rainbow Warrior,* Maori artifacts, pioneer relics, and an ancient Maori *pa.* To get there follow River Road, then turn right on Mahuta Road and follow the signs.

For self-contained accommodations, free wireless Internet, and a swimming pool, make reservations at the **Parkview Motel** (36 Carrington St., 09/439-8338, www. parkviewdargaville.co.nz, $90–130 s or d). Only a short walk from the center of town, **Greenhouse Hostel** (13 Portland St. at Gordon St., 09/439-6342, dorm beds $28, $70 s or d) is clean and friendly, and offers plenty of room to move around. The outdoor swimming pool is a bonus. Simple **Baylys Beach Motor Camp** (24 Seaview Rd., 09/439-6349, www.baylys-beach.co.nz, campsites $16 per person, cabins $75–120 s or d) is just a short walk from an unspoiled beach. The turnoff is three km (2 mi) north of Dargaville along Baylys Coast Road.

◖ Kauri Museum

From Dargaville, Highway 12 continues south along the Wairoa River to **Ruawai,** then veers inland to the small village of Matakohe and the Kauri Museum (5 Church Rd., 09/431-7417; Nov.–Apr. daily 8:30 A.M.–5:30 P.M., May–Oct. daily 9 A.M.–5 P.M.; adult $25, senior $20, child $8), which contains almost everything you'd want to know about kauri trees and gum. You'll see kauri timber, an outstanding kauri gum collection, furniture, wood flowers, old photos of lumberjacks, kauri-processing equipment, historic chainsaws, and a reproduction of a colonial cottage done entirely in kauri. Volunteers Hall houses a slab of kauri from a tree milled by the landowners after it was struck by lightning in 1986. On the wall behind, this massive tree is compared to those still standing in the forest and to the largest kauri on record. Also in this section is "Transition Gateway," sculpted from a kauri log that was underground for an estimated 30,000 years. Another room is paneled in all the different types of timber available in New Zealand. At the gift shop you can pick up beautifully crafted kauri products at reasonable prices, while across the road a café is open daily for breakfast and lunch.

SOUTH TO AUCKLAND VIA HIGHWAY 16

Highways 12 and 1 intersect at Brynderwyn, where Highway 1 continues south to Wellsford and on down to Auckland. An alternate scenic route south, Highway 16 via Helensville, branches west at Wellsford, skirting Kaipara Harbour.

Helensville and Parakai

The Helensville area, less than an hour's drive north of Auckland, boasts gentle countryside, many poultry and deer farms, and orchards and vineyards; in summer, wildflowers line the highways.

If you like hot pools and masses of people, head northwest out of Helensville along South Head Road to the town of Parakai,

© ANDREW HEMPSTEAD

gannet colony, Muriwai Beach

where you'll find **Parakai Springs** (corner of Parkhurst and Spring Rds., 09/420-8998; daily 10 A.M.–9 P.M.; adult $18, senior $12, child $9). Thermal mineral springs naturally heat the indoor and outdoor pools, so the temperatures vary a little each day—generally the outdoor pool is about 32°C (90°F), the indoor a sizzling 40°C (104°F). If you fancy the use of a private spa pool, the cost is an extra $8 per hour.

Next to Parakai Springs is **Parakai Springs Camping Ground** (09/420-8998), where camping is a reasonable $14 per person, or you can add swimming until noon the day of departure for an even more reasonable total fee of $20 per person per night. If you need a roof over your head, consider **Mineral Park Motel** (3 Parakai Ave., 09/420-8856, www.mineralparkmotel.co.nz, $130–165 s or d), where each of the eight self-contained rooms features a private outdoor mineral pool.

◖ Muriwai Beach

South of Helensville, the only worthwhile detour before reaching Auckland is Muriwai Beach, a small village at the southern end of a windswept beach. To access Muriwai, turn off Highway 16 at Waimauku. Apart from the town's laidback atmosphere, nesting Australasian gannets are the main draw. Offshore lies **Motutara Island,** where the gannets began nesting 20 years ago. The colony grew, spread to the mainland, and now numbers more than 1,200 nesting pairs. Barriers and two viewing platforms on the headland allow easy observation without disturbing the birds. The township is also home to **Muriwai Beach Motor Camp** (09/411-9262, www.muriwaimotorcamp.co.nz, $14 tent sites, $28 power sites), a general store with hot takeout food, and a golf course.

NORTHLAND

WAIKATO, COROMANDEL, AND THE BAY OF PLENTY

This region covers a wide swathe of the North Island immediately south of Auckland, extending from the Tasman Sea in the west to the Pacific Ocean in the east. The region's largest city is Hamilton, a bustling metropolis renowned for its museum and gardens. Lush green fields dotted with dairy cows that stretch away from Hamilton in all directions are part of the Waikato Plains, one of the most productive dairying and agricultural districts in New Zealand.

To see the Central North Island's best-known tourist attraction, you'll have to descend underground to the Waitomo Caves. In keeping with the entrepreneurial spirit evident around the country, the advertising will have you believe you can't complete the "Waitomo Experience" without parting with a pile of cash. Aside from touring famous Waitomo Caves and its glowworms, you can go black-water (underground) rafting, abseiling (rappelling) into a limestone shaft and cave system, horseback riding, you name it.

East of Hamilton, the Coromandel Peninsula has survived the same land exploitation as the far north. It has seen both poverty and prosperity, as well as a dramatically fluctuating population during the last 200 years, including a mass influx of miners after gold was discovered in 1852. Today the Coromandel Peninsula is again a quiet and peaceful place, recognized for its great beauty and value as a wilderness area. The small permanent population is scattered mainly

HIGHLIGHTS

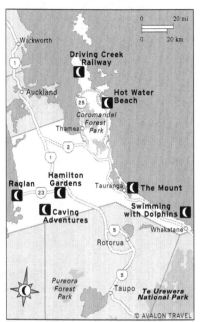

LOOK FOR **◖** TO FIND RECOMMENDED SIGHTS, ACTIVITIES, DINING, AND LODGING.

◖ Hamilton Gardens: From native forests to Japanese gardens, it's easy to spend half a day exploring this sprawling riverfront garden; best of all, the entry is free (page 92).

◖ Raglan: New Zealand's quintessential surf town comes complete with world-class waves and a laidback attitude to boot (page 97).

◖ Caving Adventures: You could explore Waitomo Caves on foot, but this is New Zealand, so you'll be expected to swim, rappel, and raft through the dark unknown (page 101).

◖ Driving Creek Railway: One man's mission is complete, and today you can ride this narrow-gauge railway to a stunning lookout point high above the forest canopy (page 107).

◖ Hot Water Beach: The spring water that seeps up through the sand makes for an all-natural hot tub. Bring your own spade and start digging (page 112).

◖ The Mount: This dormant volcano rising from the end of the beach at Mount Maunganui offers hot saltwater pools at its base and 360-degree views from its summit (page 120).

◖ Swimming with Dolphins: The dolphins off Whakatane encountered the first humans who suited up for this once-in-a-lifetime experience, which has become a New Zealand specialty (page 123).

along the coastline. Although a few of the most easily reached towns (mostly along the east coast) are rapidly becoming tourist attractions, don't let the tricky gravel roads and steepness of the terrain prevent you from discovering the more beautiful, wild side of the Coromandel.

If you're hankering for a few lazy days when the only work you do is on your tan, or if you want to try your hand at various water sports, the Coromandel Peninsula has plenty to offer. However, if you're short on time and crave tourist attractions, evening action, and tons of people, you may be happier heading directly

for Rotorua. Facing due north, the magnificent crescent-shaped Bay of Plenty stretches from the Coromandel Peninsula in the west to Cape Runaway in the east. It includes several small islands, and is backed by the Kaimai and Raukumara Ranges to the south. With its mild climate, broad sweeps of golden sand, and crystal-clear waters, the bay attracts thousands of vacationing New Zealanders during the summer and reverts to a quiet resort area in winter. The fertile land produces a large variety of subtropical fruit—including kiwifruit, feijoas, and tamarillos—and is well known for its citrus

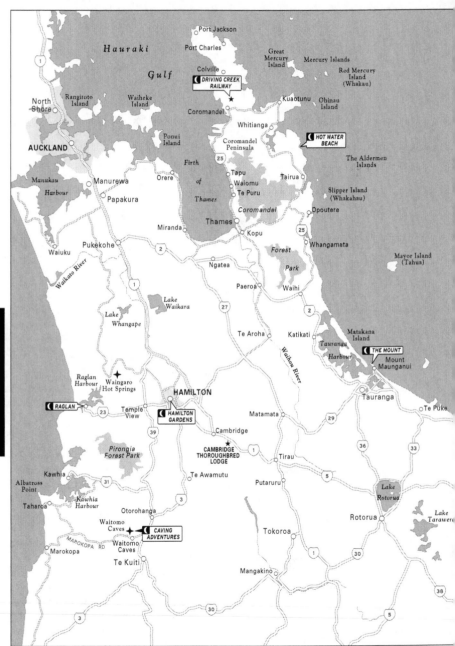

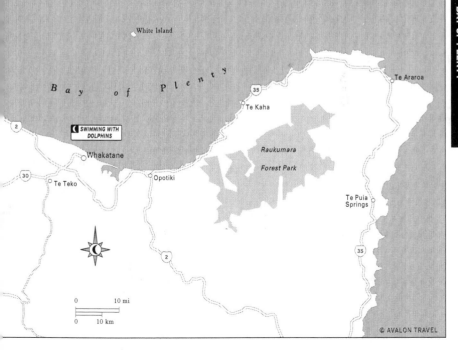

WAIKATO, COROMANDEL, AND THE BAY OF PLENTY

P A C I F I C

O C E A N

White Island

B a y   o f   P l e n t y

Te Araroa

35

Te Kaha

SWIMMING WITH DOLPHINS

Raukumara

Forest Park

Whakatane

30

Te Teko

Opotiki

2

Te Puia
Springs

35

2

0   10 mi

0   10 km

© AVALON TRAVEL

orchards, which supply a quarter of the country's total fruit crop.

PLANNING YOUR TIME

Travelers in a hurry zip south from Auckland to Rotorua, and if you have only two weeks to explore the entire country, you should too, maybe taking an hour or so out of your schedule in Hamilton to wander through **Hamilton Gardens.** Caving adventures are the main draw at **Waitomo Caves,** and adventurous souls should set aside a half day here. This region's east coast has the best beaches, but to the west, **Raglan** is renowned by surfers for its long point break. To the east of Hamilton is the Coromandel Peninsula. Seemingly lost in time, this chunk of land is mostly wilderness, with a few small towns, such as Coromandel, where an industrious potter has developed the **Driving Creek Railway.** The peninsula's east coast is all about a beachy lifestyle. Long sandy beaches, lots of sunshine, and a string of touristy towns make this region popular with New Zealanders on vacation. Aside from simply relaxing, there are a number of natural attractions worth investigating, none more unusual than **Hot Water Beach,** where you can dig your own hot pool in the sand. Volcanic in origin, **The Mount** is a local landmark overlooking fine swimming and surfing beaches, while **swimming with dolphins** is the highlight of a trip to Whakatane.

Hamilton and the Waikato

Travelers often miss Hamilton (pop. 175,000), center of the Waikato region and New Zealand's fourth largest city, in the rush to get down to Rotorua or back to Auckland. It's on Highway 1, less than 130 km (81 mi) south of Auckland and on all public transportation routes. The city itself offers the visitor many attractions and is an ideal base for exploring the coast near Raglan, intriguing Waitomo Caves, and the area's several forest park reserves. The Waikato River, originally the main shipping route between Hamilton and Auckland, meanders through the inner city, and along its banks are numerous parks and gardens. The east and west banks are connected by five city bridges, and footpaths run along the river on both sides. The city started out as a fairly small Maori village, Kirikiriroa, on the west bank of the Waikato.

The first European settlement was a military camp established in 1864, and the resulting town was named after a navy officer killed in the Battle of Gate Pa at Tauranga the same year. Hamilton has grown rapidly over the years and is now New Zealand's largest inland city.

SIGHTS AND RECREATION
Waikato Museum

This modern five-level architectural marvel (1 Grantham St., corner of Victoria St., 07/838-6606; daily 10 A.M.–4:30 P.M.; donation) sits beside the Waikato River (great water views from the upper level) and features Maori artifacts and sculptures, the fabulous 150-year-old carved war canoe *Te Winika,* contemporary Tainui carvings, Tukutuku weaving, and fine art exhibits, along with changing exhibitions. Part of the museum complex is the **Exscite Centre** (adult $6.40, child $5.30), a large hands-on interactive science center. Don't miss the aerial sculpture, *Ripples,* which hangs between the trees outside (best viewed from the River Gallery inside). It accurately represents a pebble dropping in water—a suspended moment in time. In the museum shop pick up some high-quality arts and crafts, posters, prints, books, and art cards. Adjoining the museum is one of Hamilton's best restaurants, Canvas.

◖ Hamilton Gardens
No visitor to Hamilton should miss this garden

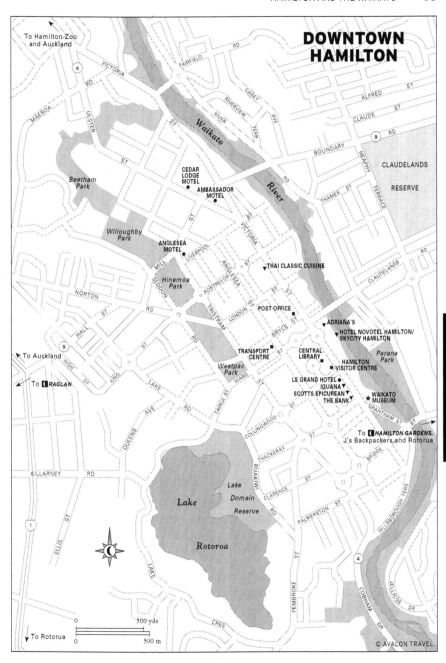

DOWNTOWN HAMILTON

BAY OF PLENTY

© ANDREW HEMPSTEAD

Hamilton Gardens is a highlight of the central North Island's largest city.

(Cobham Dr., summer daily 7:30 A.M.–8 P.M., the rest of the year daily 7:30 A.M.–6 P.M.), and not just because entry is free. Masses of roses, chrysanthemums, daffodils, camellias, magnolias, and rhododendrons; vegetable gardens; a perfume garden; trees that burst into brilliant color in autumn; and display houses sheltering tropical plants, cacti, succulents, bromeliads, and insectivorous plants can all be found throughout the 58-hectare (143-acre) grounds. The arrangement is subtle, with the Paradise Garden Collection comprising six gardens from around the world showing different perspectives on "perfection"—everything from a Japanese garden to American Modernist. A native garden is framed by an intricately carved *waharoa* (gateway), while down along the river is Echo Bank Bush, a native forest. The garden is south of downtown off Grey Street (Hwy. 1) toward Rotorua.

Hamilton Zoo

A place to appreciate a wide variety of animals is the 20-hectare (49-acre) Hamilton Zoo (Brymer Rd., north of the city, 07/838-6720; daily 9 A.M.–5 P.M.; $16 adult, $12 senior, $8 child). The main theme is conservation, and rare birds and animals are held here to establish breeding colonies, including many in a "free flight" sanctuary, where trails lead through a massive bird-filled aviary. Also on display are animals from around the world, including an ever-growing African collection.

Walking Trails

The city has three circular walking routes (brochures available at the visitor center). The **Short Historic and Scenic Walk** leads along Victoria Street, crosses Victoria Bridge, and returns along the River Walk route. The entire trip takes about 1.5 hours. The scenic three-to four-hour **River Walk,** also known as Five Bridges Walk, runs along the banks of the Waikato River. It starts from beyond Fairfield Bridge in the north and runs beyond Cobham

Bridge in the south, links all five bridges, and takes in several parks and some of the older residential streets. The **One-day Scenic Walk** covers much of the River Walk route but includes several more parks and the delightful grounds around Hamilton Lake; it takes five to eight hours to complete.

Karamu Walkway is a good track for panoramic views of Hamilton, Mount Pirongia (961 meters/3150 ft), Kakepuku, and Raglan. The northern end of the track starts at the eastern corner of the Four Brothers Scenic Reserve, almost at the top of the Kapamahunga Range. Take the Hamilton-Raglan Road (Hwy. 23) to the reserve. The track finishes 10 km (six mi) south of Whatawhata on Limeworks Road in Karamu, and takes about four hours; as a shorter alternative, you can walk the section between Four Brothers Scenic Reserve and Old Mountain Road in an hour.

ENTERTAINMENT

The most popular of several theaters offering live entertainment is the **Riverlea Theatre** (80 Riverlea Rd., Hillcrest, 07/856-5450), off Highway 1 southeast of downtown. The season runs April–October; check the website (www.riverlea.org.nz) for a schedule.

SkyCity Hamilton (346 Victoria St., 07/834-4900, www.skycityhamilton.co.nz) is a large downtown entertainment complex facing the river. Within its modern walls are a casino, a bowling alley, three bars, and a restaurant. One of the bars, **Number Eight,** opens to a riverfront balcony and has a good-value happy hour daily 5–7 P.M. Within Hamilton's most stylish boutique hotel, **Leonardo's** (Le Grand Hotel, corner of Collingwood and Victoria Sts., 07/839-1994; closed Sun.) is a good choice for a quiet drink in a refined setting.

Many pubs around Hamilton have live music Wednesday–Saturday night, with cover charges at most venues on Friday and Saturday night. Named for its location in an imposing

1879 bank, **The Bank** (corner of Victoria and Hood Sts., 07/839-4740; Sun.–Fri. 11:30 A.M.–11 P.M., Sat. 11:30 A.M.–3 A.M.) is a popular drinking spot that comes alive with live and DJ music after 10 P.M. During happy hour, weekdays 4:30–6:30 P.M., beers are just $5 each. Across the road, the **Outback** (141 Victoria St., 07/839-6354) is a massive space capable of holding 1,600 patrons in a variety of bars and dance floors. It is aimed at the local student population, attracting a younger crowd to its frenzied dance floor.

ACCOMMODATIONS AND CAMPING

J's Backpackers (8 Grey St., 07/856-8934, www.jsbackbackpackers.co.nz, dorm beds $25, $50–60 s, $54–60 d; Victoria St., 838-2704, dorm beds $25–28, $45 s, $58 d) is on the east side of the Waikato River and within walking distance of Hamilton Gardens. Rooms are on the small side, but the atmosphere is congenial, there's an outdoor barbecue area, use of bikes is free, and it's usually not that busy.

Most of Hamilton's 40-odd motels are on the fringes of the city, many concentrated along Ulster Street, the main route north out of the city (but bypassed by Hwy. 1). A good cheapie along this strip is **Cedar Lodge Motel** (174 Ulster St., 07/839-5569 or 0800/105-252, www.cedarlodge.co.nz, $95–150 s or d). Most of the 11 guest rooms have kitchens, and there's an oversized indoor spa pool and game room.

Ambassador Motel (86 Ulster St., 07/839-5111 or 0800/800-533, www.theambassador.co.nz, $135–205 s or d) is a 49-room, five-story motel close to downtown. All rooms have a kitchen, and facilities include an outdoor swimming pool and a barbecue area.

Set around a courtyard and pool, **Anglesea Motel** (corner of Liverpool and Tristram Sts., 07/834-0010 or 0800/426-453, www.angleseamotel.com, $145–240 s or d) is near the downtown end of Ulster Street. All 42 units are a little plain, but are practical and spacious, and the laundry and wireless Internet access are included in the rates.

In the heart of downtown, you'll find **Le Grand Hotel** (corner of Collingwood and Victoria Sts., 07/839-1994, www.legrandhotel.co.nz, $219–349) in a historic four-story building with a restaurant and bar and wireless Internet throughout. The large rooms have an elegant Victorian charm; ignore the rack rate and expect to pay from $130 online.

Part of the SkyCity complex, **Hotel Novotel Hamilton** (7 Alma St., 07/838-1366, www.novotel.com, from $250 s or d) is a full-service hotel with 177 rooms and all the conveniences expected (restaurant, bar, valet parking, 24-hour room service).

Holiday Park

On the eastern side of the city is **Hamilton City Holiday Park** (14 Ruakura Rd., Hamilton East, 07/855-8255, www.hamiltoncityholidaypark.co.nz, camping $35, dorm beds $32, cabins $70–110 s or d), where each campsite is surrounded by a high hedge. To get there, cross the central downtown bridge at Claudelands Road, turn right on Grey Street, and then turn left on Te Aroha Street. At the Peachgrove Road intersection, continue straight onto Ruakura Road.

FOOD

Kick-start your day with a healthy breakfast at ◖**Scotts Epicurean** (181 Victoria St., 07/839-6680; Mon.–Fri. 7 A.M.–5 P.M., Sat.–Sun. 8:30 A.M.–5 P.M.; $9–18), for both wonderful food and a welcoming ambience. At breakfast, you could order muesli with fresh fruit and yogurt, while at lunch the classically simple aglio olio is a good choice.

Opening to a large courtyard, the **Curio Café** (Waikato Museum, 1 Grantham St., 07/839-1921; daily 10 A.M.–4:30 P.M.; $8–16) has premade sandwiches and salads, as well as a few simple lunch dishes.

Within Hamilton Gardens, **Garden Café** (Cobham Dr., 07/856-6581; daily 9:30 A.M.–5 P.M., until 6 P.M. in summer; $9–17) is a delightful lunch spot, especially on warm days when outside tables are set out beside a large pond. As you would expect in such a setting, the food is light and healthy, with salads and wraps dominating the menu.

Hip **Iguana** (203 Victoria St., 07/834-2280; Mon.–Fri. 10 A.M.–10 P.M., Sat.–Sun. 10 A.M.–3 A.M.; $22–34) is a vast dining area with seating that ranges from bar stools to couches. The menu might not be groundbreaking in Auckland, but in Hamilton, ordering pizza topped with prawns and beef is definitely out of the ordinary. The kitchen demonstrates its worldliness by using real bacon and anchovies in the Caesar salad.

For a touristy casino, the food at **Rebo Restaurant** (SkyCity Hamilton, 346 Victoria St., 07/834-4925; daily 11 A.M.–11 P.M.; $24–34) is surprisingly good. Build-your-own platters are perfect to share, or enjoy mains such as salmon baked in a chili-mint crust. Also within the casino is **Silk** (daily 11 A.M.–11 P.M.; $18–26), a contemporary restaurant featuring classic dishes from throughout Asia.

Off Victoria Street, along the access road to SkyCity, is **Adriana's** (6 Alma St., 07/838-0370; Mon.–Sat. from 6 P.M.; $21–32), a small Italian restaurant with an orange color theme extending from the facade to the tablecloths. Portions of dishes such as *gnocchi al salmone* (potato dumplings with smoked salmon, spinach, and cream sauce) are generous, although prices are a little higher than at other local restaurants.

At the far northern end of town is **Thai Classic Cuisine** (783 Victoria St., 07/839-3626; daily 5–10:30 P.M.; $15–24), with a traditional Thai feel (think Buddha statues and gold-framed paintings). Mains, such as a creamy green curry, are mostly under $20.

INFORMATION AND SERVICES

Hamilton Visitor Centre (5 Garden Place, 07/958-5960, www.visithamilton.com, Mon.–Fri. 9 A.M.–5 P.M., Sat.–Sun.

9:30 A.M.–3:30 P.M.) is in the heart of downtown, just off Victoria Street.

The 200,000-book-strong **Garden Place Library** (9 Garden Place, 07/838-6826; Mon.–Fri. 9 A.M.–8:30 P.M., Sat. 9 A.M.–4 P.M., Sun. noon–3:30 P.M.) is the largest and most centrally located of six libraries in Hamilton. The main post office is at 36 Bryce Street. Both the library and visitor center have Internet access. **Waikato Hospital** is on Pembroke Street (07/839-8899). For non-emergencies, go to the **Victoria Central Medical Centre** (750 Victoria St., 07/834-0333; daily 8 A.M.–10 P.M.).

GETTING THERE AND AROUND

Air, bus, and rail services converge on the city. **Hamilton International Airport** (www.hamiltonairport.co.nz) is 13 km (eight mi) south of the city and is linked to downtown by the **Super Shuttle** (07/843-7778; $15 door-to-door). **Air New Zealand** (0800/737-000, www.airnewzealand.com) has direct flights from Hamilton to Auckland, Wellington, Christchurch, and Dunedin. One train a day in each direction stops at **Hamilton Railway Station** (Fraser St.) on the Auckland–Wellington route.

Go to the **Transport Centre** (corner of Ward and Anglesea Sts.) for **Intercity** (07/834-3457, www.intercity.co.nz) buses to and from throughout the North Island. The center has a café, Internet access, and lockers.

Busit! (07/846-1975) buses head throughout the city from the Transport Centre (corner of Ward and Anglesea Sts.), which also serves as the main visitor center and long-distance bus depot. Tickets are $2.30 per sector or $7 for a day pass. Car rental agencies in Hamilton include **Budget** (07/838-3585) and **Rent-a-dent** (07/839-1049).

Cabs wait outside the Transport Centre, or call **Combined Taxi** (07/839-9099) or **Hamilton Taxis** (07/447-7477).

WAINGARO HOT SPRINGS

The sulphur-free bubbling waters of this thermal spring (Waingaro Rd., 07/825-4761,

www.waingarohotsprings.co.nz; daily 9 A.M.–9:30 P.M.; adult $11, child $6), 42 km (26 mi) northwest of Hamilton, have been diverted into three concrete pools and down a hot-water water slide. The temperatures range 30–42°C (86–108°F). The sprawling grounds include a campground (campsites $21 per person, cabins $80 s or d, motel rooms $115) where rates include pool admission. If you're coming from the north, save some time and head directly for Waingaro. This allows you to take in both the hot springs and Raglan area attractions before reaching Hamilton. Turn west off Highway 1 at Ngaruawahia toward Glen Massey. Before Glen Massey turn right heading for Te Akatea, continue to the Waingaro River, and turn left toward Waingaro. If you're already in Hamilton, head west along Highway 23 toward Raglan, then take Highway 22 north and continue to Waingaro Hot Springs.

◼ RAGLAN

Renowned as one of the world's greatest surfing spots, Raglan (pop. 2,600) lies 48 km (30 mi) west of Hamilton along Highway 23 at the mouth of Raglan Harbour. It is the nearest coastal resort to Hamilton, but is passed over by most sun-seekers due to its lack of golden sandy beaches. Most of the year, it's a quiet little seaside town, but in summer it gets quite busy.

Sights and Recreation

Surfing takes place west of Raglan at breaks scattered along the coast. When the swell is up and the conditions are right, the breaks link up to form one of the world's longest left-hand point breaks. As Wainui Road winds southwest around the coast, it passes a number of spectacular lookouts before descending to **Manu Bay** and a grassy area perfect for relaxing and watching the surfing action. Continuing westward, the road passes through the small community of **Whale Bay,** another popular surfing spot with the renowned breaks of Indicators,

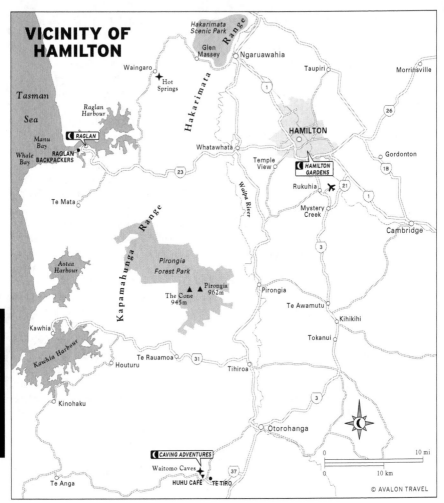

VICINITY OF HAMILTON

Hakarimata Scenic Park

Hakarimata Range

Glen Massey

Ngaruawahia

Waingaro

Hot Springs

Taupiri

Morrinsville

Tasman

Sea

Raglan Harbour

HAMILTON

26

Manu Bay

RAGLAN

Whatawhata

Whale Bay

RAGLAN BACKPACKERS

Hakarimata Range

Temple View

HAMILTON GARDENS

Gordonton

1B

Te Mata

23

Rukuhia

21

1

Waipa River

Mystery Creek

Cambridge

Kapamahunga Range

Aotea Harbour

Pirongia Forest Park

Pirongia 962m

Pirongia

The Cone 945m

3

Te Awamutu

Kawhia

Kihikihi

Tokanui

Kawhia Harbour

Te Rauamoa

31

Houturu

Tihiroa

Kinohaku

3

Otorohanga

0   10 mi

0   10 km

CAVING ADVENTURES

Waitomo Caves

Te Anga

HUHU CAFÉ   TE TIRO

37

© AVALON TRAVEL

the Valley, and Outsides. Raglan also has good harbor and surf fishing, and whitebait fishing in the local streams.

South of Raglan along the inland roads, pass through Te Mata to reach the spectacular **Bridal Veil Falls** near Lake Disappear, 21 km (13 mi) southeast of Raglan off the main road to Kawhia. Walk about 10 minutes along a bush trail to emerge at a thundering torrent of water plummeting 60 meters (197 ft) down a lava rock face into a deep pool, a popular swimming hole in summer. For an even more dramatic view, continue for another 10 minutes down the steep track to the base of the falls.

Practicalities

One of my favorite budget accommodations in New Zealand is **Raglan Backpackers** (6 Wi Neera St., 07/825-0515, www.raglanbackpackers.co.nz, dorm beds $27–29, $57 s, $72

© ANDREW HEMPSTEAD

Surfing is the main activity at Raglan.

d). This purpose-built budget accommodation lies right on Raglan Harbour and just 100 meters (330 ft) from the main street. The rooms all open to a large courtyard, complete with outdoor furniture and hammocks, while the spotless kitchen and cozy lounge overlook the harbor. There's a large selection of recreational equipment for guest use, including surfboards ($30 per day) and wet suits, canoes, bikes, and fishing tackle. The old hotel on the main street, **Harbour View Hotel** (14 Bow St., 07/825-8010, $70 s, $90 d) offers seven basic rooms. Or stay at **Raglan Kopua Holiday Park** (Marine Pde., 07/825-8283, www.raglanholidaypark.co.nz, campsites $32–34, cabins from $85 s or d), across an arm of the harbor from downtown but linked by a pedestrian bridge. Overlooking the surf break, **Whale Bay Surf Bach** (9 Tohora Close, Whale Bay, 07/825-8219, www.whalebaysurf.co.nz, $200 for the entire house) is a small beach house that sleeps four in two bedrooms. It has a wonderful oceanfront location,

a kitchen, and a grassed area out front for watching the surf.

The Hawaiian-born owner of **Vinnies** (7 Wainui Rd., 07/825-7273; Tues.–Sun. 8 A.M.–10 P.M.), legendary in this part of the world, offers an informal atmosphere and a blackboard menu with a bit of everything—Mexican, Thai, Italian, and more. It's a great place to just hang out, and anyone who has sampled the food keeps coming back for more. Free wireless Internet is a bonus. On the main street, trendy little **Tongue and Groove** café (19 Bow St., 07/825-0027; Mon.–Thurs. 8:30 A.M.–3 P.M., Fri.–Sun. 8:30 A.M.–8:30 P.M.; $10–19) serves up a wide variety of coffee drinks, and well-prepared cooked breakfasts.

Raglan Information Centre (12 Wainui Rd., 07/825-0556, www.raglan.org.nz, Mon.–Thurs. 9:30 A.M.–4:30 P.M., Fri. 9:30 A.M.–5 P.M., Sat. 10 A.M.–5 P.M.) is in the center of town.

CAMBRIDGE

If you've been through rural England, Cambridge (pop. 13,000), 20 km (12 mi) southeast of Hamilton on Highway 1, will bring back memories of tree-lined avenues, immaculate flower-filled gardens, old buildings, and the traditional village green. The jade-green Waikato River runs through this scenic town, and the streets are bordered by abundant varieties of trees that meet overhead in a lush colorful archway (spectacular in late April and May, when they take on brilliant autumnal colors).

Cambridge Thoroughbred Lodge

Between Hamilton and Cambridge you'll see field after field of racehorses intermingled with stud stables, which cater to an international yearling market. One of the most prominent operations is Cambridge Thoroughbred Lodge (six km/3.7 mi southeast of Cambridge on Hwy. 1, 07/827-8118; Mon.–Fri. 10 A.M.–2 P.M.), which in addition to training some of the world's fastest racehorses hosts an exhibition called New Zealand Horse Magic (adult $12, child $5). It's an entertaining and informative show—and a good value for equestrian types. Call for show times (usually twice weekly through summer).

Practicalities

Cambridge Mews (20 Hamilton Rd., 07/827-7166, www.cambridgemews.co.nz, $155–190 s or d) is an upscale motel with 12 spacious rooms, each with a kitchen, a writing desk, and a bathroom with separate shower and spa bath. It's along Highway 1 on the north side of town.

While you're in Cambridge, be sure to sample breakfast, morning or afternoon tea, or a light lunch at **Toccata Café** (Mon.–Sat. 8:30 A.M.–5 P.M., Sun. 9 A.M.–5 P.M.; lunches $9–16) above **Cambridge Country Store** (92 Victoria St., 07/827-7100). You can't miss the two-story orange-red building. The café has a large variety of assorted hot dishes,

sandwiches, and salads, and the dessert specialty (among many tantalizers) is delicious orange cheesecake.

Cambridge Visitor Centre (corner of Victoria and Queen Sts., 07/823-3456, www.cambridge.co.nz, Mon.–Fri. 10 A.M.–3 P.M., Sat.–Sun. 10 A.M.–4 P.M.) is in the town hall building.

WAITOMO CAVES AND VICINITY

Waitomo, 70 km (44 mi) south of Hamilton and eight km (five mi) west off Highway 3, is most famous for its caves, but it has gained a reputation in recent years as the adventure capital of the North Island. This entire area is part of an ancient seabed that was lifted by enormous pressures from deep below the Earth's surface. Then erosion took over, with water action creating a complex system of caves, some with rivers flowing through them, others decorated with natural wonders such as stalactites.

Waitomo Caves Discovery Centre

Start exploration at the intriguing Waitomo Caves Discovery Centre (39 Waitomo Caves Rd., 07/878-7640, www.waitomo-museum.co.nz, summer daily 8:45 A.M.–5:30 P.M., the rest of the year daily 8:45 A.M.–5 P.M.; adult $10). This puts you in the mood for all the other activities and gives you as much background knowledge as you desire. Displays feature local geology, flora and fauna, spelunking, fossils, surveying know-how, skeletal remains found in nearby caves, the history of tourism in the area, preserved birds, insects, and glowworms. Don't miss the excellent audiovisual program on spelunking. The building also houses the local information center. Entry to the museum is free with paid admission to Glowworm or Aranui Caves.

The Caves

Many of the Waitomo caves are accessible only by joining a caving adventure, but three are open to the public for general viewing on

GLOWWORMS

Glowworms, New Zealand's fairy lights, twinkle by the thousands in caves and other moist and shady places, much to the wonderment of humans. The larva of a luminous gnat, the glowworm is a tiny fisherman that suspends itself from a cave ceiling or other canopy with fine, silky, sticky threads one to five cm long. Its tail end glows bluish-green, more brightly the hungrier it gets. It preys on bugs that breed in the mudbanks and water below the glowworm; they fly toward the light and entangle themselves in the glowworm's net. The glowworm hauls up the lines and feasts on the trapped bugs.

Proceed with caution when you enter the glowworms' grottoes. They don't like loud noise; one clap and all the lights go out. They don't like bright light; shine a torch on them and the twinkles will fade. And hands off; they are fragile, and a human touch will kill them.

a guided tour. The main attraction within **Glowworm Cave** is the magical glowworm grotto. Quietly glide through the water-filled grotto in a boat, gazing upward at the vast ceiling of twinkling lights. Tours through Glowworm Cave are run daily, generally every 30 minutes 9 A.M.–5 P.M., with extra tours at 5:30 P.M. in peak periods. Photography is not allowed in this cave. The entrance is 500 meters (0.3 mi) west of the Waitomo Visitor Centre. Farther along the road, **Aranui Cave** is definitely the more beautiful of the two caves, but lacks water and therefore there are no glowworms. The pink and white limestone formations are exquisite. Tours leave on the hour 10 A.M.–3 P.M. from the cave entrance. Both tours take 45 minutes and cost adult $48, child $21 (or pay adult $65, child $29 for a combined ticket). No reservations are necessary and tickets can be bought from the booth at Glowworm Cave (39 Waitomo Caves Rd., 07/878-8228).

Known to the local Maori for over 500 years as the "Den of Dogs," but only recently opened to the public, the 1.6-km (one-mi) walking tour of **Ruakuri Cave** is more strenuous than the above tours. The entrance to the cave is a Maori burial site, so access is via a vertical passageway lined by a spiral staircase. Tours leave from the **Black Water Rafting Co.** (585 Waitamo Caves Rd., 07/878-5903) six times daily, last about two hours, and cost adult $67, child $26.

◖ Caving Adventures

Black-water rafting began in New Zealand in the mid-1980s. It's offered at locations throughout the country, but the Waitomo experience is the original and still the best. It involves donning wet suits and helmets with headlamps, plunging into the Huhunui stream on an inner tube, and drifting along an underground river for about 90 minutes. In some places you need to get off and scramble, and in Ruakuri Cave, jump down a waterfall. Afterward a hot shower and a snack are provided. All you need to take is a swimsuit (wear it), a towel, socks, running shoes, and a waterproof camera with flash. The tour departs up to eight times daily from the **Legendary Black Water Rafting Co.** complex (585 Waitamo Caves Rd., 07/878-5903 or 0800/228-464, www.waitomo.com, $119 per person), 1.2 km (one mi) east of Waitomo village. This company offers other adventures, including Black Abyss ($220), a five-hour journey that begins with a rappel into the cave.

Competing for your tourist dollar is **Waitomo Adventures** (07/878-7788 or 0800/924-8666, www.waitomo.co.nz), best known for Lost World Epic. This adventure involves abseiling 100 meters (330 ft) into a limestone cave to see gold-colored stalactites, waterfalls, and glowworms. Once you reach the base of the cave, lunch is served; then it's upstream, wading, walking, swimming, and climbing through caves, vaults, and valleys to get back out. The seven-hour trip is truly an incredible experience, one that will be a highlight of your stay in New Zealand—and anyone of a reasonable fitness level can do it. The minimum age is 15 and the cost is $455 per person.

Otorohanga Kiwi House

Otorohanga, the nearest town to Waitomo, is worth a stop for the Otorohanga Kiwi House (Alex Telfer Dr., 07/873-7391; daily 9 A.M.–4:30 P.M.; adult $20, child $6), filling a valley surrounded by homes. Here you can see kiwis in the nocturnal house, walk through an enormous aviary, and watch New Zealand's rare and unusual birds and reptiles in their natural habitat.

Accommodations and Camping

Kiwi Paka Waitomo (Hotel Access Rd., 07/878-3395, www.kiwipaka.co.nz, dorm beds $30, $65 s, $70 d, chalet $110–150 s or d) is a large, modern complex directly behind the museum and information center. If you don't feel like cooking in the communal kitchen, there's a great pizza restaurant on-site, as well as the usual communal facilities. Accommodation options include dorms and private rooms, but the best value is the beautiful chalets with en suite bathrooms.

Another backpacker lodge within walking distance of everything is **YHA Waitomo Juno Hall** (600 Waitomo Caves Rd., 07/878-7649, www.junowaitomo.co.nz, dorm beds $28, $75 s or d), one km (0.6 mi) east of the information center. It's a well-run operation, with a swimming pool, tennis court, and horseback riding.

As two of the original black-water rafting guides, your hosts at (**Te Tiro** (970 Caves–Te Anga Rd., 07/878-6328, www.waitomocavesnz.com, $90 s, $120 d) is the perfect source of information on everything these is to see and do around the valley. Accommodation is in one of two modern wooden cottages, each with a kitchen and balcony with valley views. Set on

a farm 10 km (6.2 mi) west of Waitomo, the property even has its own glowworm grotto.

The area's only roadside motel is out on Highway 3, eight km (five mi) from the caves. **Glow Worm Motel** (07/873-8882, www.glowwormmotel.co.nz, $90–130 d) has nine self-contained units, a swimming pool, a laundry, and an adjacent restaurant.

Waitomo Top 10 Holiday Park (12 Waitomo Caves Rd., 07/878-7639 or 0508/498-666, www.waitomopark.co.nz, campsites $28, cabins $70–120 s or d, motel rooms $140–170) spreads out across the road from the village. Amenities include a communal kitchen, barbecue area, and laundry. Campsites are limited at Waitomo, so book in advance or register early in the day.

Food

As well as selling groceries and souvenirs, **Waitomo General Store** (07/878-8613; daily 7 A.M.–7 P.M.) has a small café with good pizza from $16 and a variety of other inexpensive items to eat in or take out. **Morepork Pizzeria** (Kiwi Paka Waitomo, Hotel Access Rd., 07/878-3395; 7:30 A.M.–10:30 P.M.) opens early for breakfast, but pizza is the specialty, with a medium ($24) serving two.

My favorite Waitomo eatery for a casual lunch is the **Long Black Café** (585 Waitomo Caves Rd., 07/878-7361; daily 9 A.M.–5 P.M.; $8–14), 1.2 km (one mi) east of the village. It's always filled with customers coming or going from a caving adventure. Join them for a full cooked breakfast, or a steak sandwich washed down with a milkshake. A deck overlooks the forest, and inside there is Internet access.

Make reservations at (**HUHU Café** (10 Waitomo Caves Rd., 07/878-6674; daily 4–9 P.M.; $27–35) to enjoy the best food in the Waitomo area. The casual ambience of this contemporary restaurant, which opens to a wide deck overlooking native bush, belies the high-quality cooking, much of it using local ingredients. You could start with the char-grilled zucchini salad and then choose a main such as parmesan-crusted rabbit or slow-cooked duck. Round out your meal with blueberry crumble pie. Children are not forgotten, with New Zealand favorites such as baked beans on toast and a mini lamb shoulder. The wide choice of New Zealand beer and wine is also noteworthy.

Practicalities

From the **Waitomo Visitor Centre** (Waitomo Caves Discovery Centre, 39 Waitomo Caves Rd., 07/878-8227 or 0800/456-922; summer daily 8:45 A.M.–5:30 P.M., the rest of the year daily 8:45 A.M.–5 P.M.), bookings can be made for cave tours and recreational activities, and the staff keeps a list of local bed-and-breakfasts.

Intercity (www.intercity.co.nz) stops outside the visitor center; the **Waitomo Shuttle** (07/873-8279) runs in to Waitomo from the highway. The **Waitomo Wanderer** (03/477-9083, www.waitomotours.co.nz) operates day trips from Rotorua and Taupo to Waitomo.

Marokopa Road

The narrow road west from Waitomo winds for 52 scenic km (32 mi) to the small coastal community of **Marokopa,** passing many natural wonders along the way. At the end of a 500-meter (1,640-ft) trail that begins 25 km (16 mi) from Waitomo, **Mangapohue Natural Bridge** is a massive arch spanning a small stream—it was once part of a mighty cave system. The trail passes under the bridge and leads to a bed of fossilized oysters. A few km farther west is **Piripiri Cave.** There are no cave tours, so you're on your own (bring a flashlight). Continuing west for two km (one mi), a parking lot marks the trailhead for a short (500-meter/1,640-ft) walk to **Marokopa Falls.** Cascading 30 meters (98 ft) over a limestone ledge, the falls are one of the most photogenic in the country. At the end of the road lies the fishing village of Marokopa. From the *very* end of the road, it's a pleasant 800-meter (2,625-ft) walk through black sand to the ocean. Early in the 1900s, when Marokopa was a bustling port town, many ships were lost attempting to negotiate the river mouth. The anchor from one such ship was salvaged and now sits in the parking lot at the end of the road.

BAY OF PLENTY

Coromandel Peninsula

Lying equidistant from both Hamilton and Auckland and less than two hours' drive from either is the Coromandel Peninsula, a place that no hiker or outdoor enthusiast should miss. This finger of land stretches northward from the gateway town of Thames, separating the Hauraki Gulf and Firth of Thames on the west from the Pacific Ocean in the east. Like vertebrae, the rugged mountains of the Coromandel Range snake down the center of the peninsula, supporting the 72,000 hectares (177,900 acres) of wilderness and bush that make up Coromandel Forest Park. The peninsula is an area of contrasts: Along the western shores, steep, rocky cliffs terminate abruptly at the sea, while the eastern shores offer sandy beaches and private, sheltered coves. Wherever you go on the east coast you'll find beautiful beaches. If you also want peace and quiet, and maybe your own private bush-fringed cove, stay in the north. For lots of people and the bustle of a coastal resort, head for the large towns such as Whitianga and Whangamata at the southern end of the peninsula.

THAMES AND VICINITY

After crossing the Waihou River, Highway 25 swings north to Thames (pop. 9,000), the gateway to the Coromandel Peninsula, 115 km (71 mi) from Auckland. In 1852, gold was found farther north in the area of the present town of Coromandel. It wasn't till 1867 that the Thames district was officially opened up for gold prospecting. In the next three years Thames boomed. The rush continued until 1924, and many of the old-style buildings around town are reminders of this colorful past. Before a road link was built, Thames Port used to be the peninsula's link with the outside world, and was frequented by large riverboats and cutters. Today the port is very quiet, and caters to a small fishing fleet and many recreational boats. Thames is a commercial center for surrounding farmlands and is rapidly becoming more of a tourist attraction with its gold-rush history and close proximity to Coromandel Forest Park.

Sights

At the top end of town, where Pollen Street rejoins the highway, **Goldmine Experience** (Main Rd., 07/868-8514; summer daily 10 A.M.–4 P.M., spring and fall Sat.–Sun. 10 A.M.–1 P.M.; adult $15, child $5) was the site of one of the most productive gold mines on the peninsula. You can go on an underground guided tour through a mine shaft, try gold panning, as well as see a working stamper battery, a reconstructed mine manager's office, and a small museum.

The building that houses the **Thames Historical Museum** (corner of Pollen and Cochrane Sts., 07/868-8509; summer daily 1–4 P.M.; adult $4, child $2) is more than 100 years old, and the museum features century-old printing and photographic equipment and 19th-century clothing.

Thames School of Mines and Mineralogical Museum (101 Cochrane St., 07/868-6227; summer daily 11 A.M.–8 P.M., the rest of the year Wed.–Sun. 11 A.M.–4 P.M.; adult $4, child $2) is three blocks west of the historical museum. The School of Mines was open between 1886 and

© ANDREW HEMPSTEAD

The streets of Thames are lined with historic buildings.

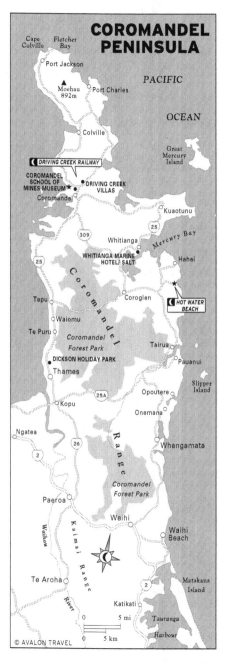

1954, teaching skills to prospective gold miners. It's now a museum, featuring an extensive collection of local and overseas mineral samples and a working model of a stamper battery (used on quartz claims to pound quartz into powder).

Coromandel Forest Park

This 73,000-hectare (180,400-acre) park, extending along the spine of the Coromandel Peninsula, protects rugged bush-clad ranges with their ancient volcanic plugs and dense remnants of kauri forest. The park is laced with hiking tracks that vary from short walks to rugged overnight tramps in mountainous backcountry. The most easily accessed section of the park is from the Kauaeranga Valley, reached by following Banks Street east out of Thames and across the Kauaeranga River. This road winds through the beautiful Kauaeranga Valley, passing several good camping areas and four short tracks, before terminating at the starting point of some of the more difficult hiking tracks.

Accommodations and Camping

Sunkist Backpackers (506 Brown St., 07/868-8808, www.sunkistbackpackers.com, camping $19 per person, dorm beds $25–29, $66 s or d) is one of Thames's appealing historic buildings left behind from gold-mining days, with a spacious upstairs verandah. Choose from dorms or single, twin, double, or triple rooms, with the use of communal bathrooms, fully equipped kitchen, dining room, TV lounge, pool table, laundry, barbecue, and garden. It's a popular place at any time of year, but there's usually room—book for January and February, especially for double rooms.

Of the many motels in and around Thames, the **Avalon Motel** (104 Jellicoe Cres., 07/868-7755, www.motelavalon.co.nz, $110–150 s or d) provides the best value, with the rates including wireless Internet. At the south end of downtown and overlooking the Kauaeranga River, the Avalon features 11 kitchen-equipped units, an indoor spa pool, a barbecue area, and a laundry.

A short walk from the center of town, **Rolleston Motel** (105 Rolleston St., 07/868-8091 or 0800/776-644, www.rollestonmotel.co.nz, $110–130 s, $95–120 d) is an older-style single-story motel with a pool, spa, and laundry. All rooms include a kitchen. **Coastal Motor Lodge** (608 Tararu Rd., 07/868-6843, www.stayatcoastal.co.nz, $120–190 s or d) backs on the forest three km (two mi) north of Thames and features spacious self-contained cottages and chalets in a lush garden setting across the road from the water.

South of town in Totara is **Cotswold Cottage** (Maramarahi Rd., 07/868-6306, www.cotswoldcottage.co.nz, $165–205 d). Right by the Kauaeranga River, a verandah offers a great view of the surrounding countryside. All three rooms include private bathrooms, and the rate includes a delicious cooked breakfast. Dinner is available for an extra $45 per person.

Also out of town, but to the north, is **La Casa Te Puru Lodge** (Hwy. 25, Te Puru, 07/868-2326, www.lacasatepurulodge.co.nz, $90–150 s or d). Well signposted from the highway, it's high on a hill overlooking the town and the Firth of Thames. This Mediterranean-style accommodation has a number of rooms fronting the extensive garden, each with a private bathroom, and three rooms that share a bathroom. Rates include wireless Internet and use of a kitchen and laundry.

Three km (two mi) north and closest to town is the excellent **◖Dickson Holiday Park** (Victoria St., 07/868-7308, www.dicksonpark.co.nz). On the grounds of an 1870s gold mine, it has a lush parklike camping area in a natural bush setting—a great spot to get away from it all and unwind, hike local trails, pan for gold in Tararu Stream, or relax at a nearby waterfall and wonderful swimming hole. In addition to the usual communal kitchen, there's a Pioneer Kitchen, a working re-creation of the rustic cooking facilities used by miners in days gone by. Other facilities include a laundry,

swimming pool, bikes, trampolines, a half-sized tennis court, and a camp office selling basics. All campsites are $39, bunkroom accommodation is $24 per person, cabins (with fridge and cooking hot plate) and on-site caravans range $60–85 s or d, tourist flats (private bathroom, kitchen, TV, and radio) are $110 s or d, and motel units are $136.

Food

You'll find the usual tearooms, takeaways, and cafés throughout Thames, mostly on mile-long Pollen Street, the main shopping street downtown. At the top end of town, **Sola Café** (720 Pollen St., 07/868-8781; daily 8:30 A.M.–4 P.M.; lunches $10.50–12.50) has an earthy color scheme and an equally warm atmosphere. The vegetation goes beyond the typical, with free-range eggs used for cooking and everything made in-house from scratch. Only one or two dishes are over $12, and options include wheat- and gluten-free choices like cheese, corn, and potato enchiladas. At breakfast, the sourdough bread smothered in Manuka honey is delicious.

Practicalities

Thames Information Centre (206 Pollen St., 07/868-7284, www.thamesinfo.co.nz, summer Mon.–Fri. 9 A.M.–5 P.M., Sat.–Sun. 10 A.M.–4 P.M., shorter hours the rest of the year) is at the south end of downtown (signposted from Hwy. 25).

The post office is on Pollen Street. **Thames Laundromat** (740 Pollen St.) doubles as an Internet café.

Departing Auckland, **Intercity** (www.intercity.co.nz) operates a daily service east to Thames. Buses stop at Thames Information Centre (206 Pollen St., 07/868-7284) before continuing north to Coromandel. Intercity also has a direct service between Thames and Rotorua. Thames is a compact little town, and you can get just about anywhere on foot. Otherwise, call **Thames Taxis** (07/868-6037).

Thames to Coromandel

From Thames, Highway 25 northbound hugs the Firth of Thames for 40 km (25 mi), then cuts across two low-lying peninsulas before reaching the small town of Coromandel. This coastal road, perhaps most beautiful in early summer when the bordering *pohutukawa* trees are ablaze with red flowers, passes by rocky outcrops, picture-perfect bays, and small beaches.

About 18 km (11 mi) north of Thames, the hamlet **Tapu** lies at the junction of Highway 25 and an unpaved road that crosses the peninsula to Whitianga. Tapu is known for its long stretch of sandy beach, shallow water, and safe swimming. Meaning "running water" to the Maori, **Rapaura** (6 km/3.7 mi east of Hwy. 25, 07/868-4821, www.rapaura.co.nz; Oct.–Apr. daily 9 A.M.–5 P.M.; adult $15, child $7.50) is a 26-hectare (64-acre) private estate that features waterfalls, fountains, and fish-filled ponds. The highlight is Seven Steps to Heaven, a trail that winds through lush forest to a small waterfall. Rapaura has a café (daily from 9 A.M.) and you can also stay overnight in one of two rooms in the main building ($275 s or d) or in a cottage ($165).

COROMANDEL AND VICINITY

A quiet fishing and crafts village 60 km north of Thames, Coromandel is particularly appealing. Despite its small size (pop. 1,500), it's the business center of the far north, offering quite a variety of services—and it's the last place (other than one store at Colville) to stock up on supplies before continuing north.

◖ Driving Creek Railway

The one Coromandel attraction, which lures many visitors up the peninsula, is Driving Creek Railway (2.5 km/1.5 mi north of town, then a short distance along Driving Creek Rd., 07/866-8703). This unique narrow-gauge mountain railway was built by Barry Brickell, a well-known New Zealand potter, to serve his potteries with clay and pine wood for fuel for the kilns in the valley below. He carved a track through the forest, laying 2.5 km (1.5 mi) of line and even building the diesel-powered train himself. Nowadays you can take a ride on the train across four bridges, around a switchback, and through two tunnels to see the native kauri forest restoration project, displays, and views across Hauraki Gulf from the Eyefull Tower. The one-hour return trip departs year-round, daily at 10:15 A.M. and 2 P.M. (additional trips in summer) and costs adult $25, senior $23, child $10. Another reason to venture out here is to browse through **Driving Creek Pottery** (daily 10 A.M.–5 P.M.), where you can buy the work of the resident potters, including homegrown wool, paper, and flax products.

Coromandel School of Mines Museum

Coromandel School of Mines Museum (841 Rings Rd., 07/866-7251; summer daily 10 A.M.–4 P.M., the rest of the year weekends only; donation) tells the story of the town, which boomed after 1852, when a logger discovered gold-bearing quartz in nearby Driving Creek. Ask here about guided tours of the nearby stamper battery, where you can see ore-crushing demonstrations for gold extraction, pan amalgamation, and plate amalgamation.

Accommodations and Camping

South off Highway 25, **Tui Lodge** (60 Whangapoua Rd., Hwy. 25, 07/866-8237; dorm beds $25, $60–80 s or d) is surrounded by grassy paddocks and citrus and macadamia orchards. If you need a ride out from town, give the owners a call and they'll collect you.

Comprising two rows of older self-contained cottages, **Coromandel Colonial Cottages Motel** (1737 Rings Rd., 07/866-8857 or 0508/222-688, www.corocottagesmotel.co.nz, $125–175 s or d) is surrounded by well-tended gardens and native bush, with a covered barbecue area and outdoor swimming pool off to one side.

Nestled high above the water and surrounded by native bush, **Buffalo Lodge** north

BAY OF PLENTY

of town (860 Buffalo Rd., 07/866-8960, www. buffalolodge.co.nz, Oct.–Apr., $235–285 s or d including breakfast) is one of the peninsula's finest accommodations. Taking advantage of its elevation, the lodge features a wide wraparound deck, with native timber dominant throughout. The four well-appointed guest rooms include thoughtful touches such as heated towel rails and plush robes. Dinner is available for an additional charge.

Overlooking the creek where New Zealand's first gold discovery was made is **❰ Driving Creek Villas** (21A Colville Rd., 07/866-7755, www.drivingcreekvillas.com, $295 s or d). The three units are brightly and practically furnished, yet remain elegant, with the private deck a perfect place to sip a morning coffee while listening to the resident birdlife.

Coromandel Top 10 Holiday Park (636 Rings Rd., 07/866-8830, www.coromandel-holidaypark.co.nz, tent sites $15 per person, powered $18 per person, cabins $75–165 s or d) has a communal bathroom, kitchen, laundry, great outdoor pool, recreation room, trampoline, and barbecue. It is one km (0.6 mi) east of town toward Colville.

Food

The local specialty is mussels. For these, as well as smoked salmon, eel, and oysters, stop by the **Coromandel Smoking Company** (70 Tiki Rd., 07/866-8793; daily 9 A.M.–5 P.M.). To enjoy mussels in a café setting, head to the **Coromandel Mussel Kitchen** (corner Manaia and 309 Rds., 07/866-7245; lunch daily; $10–17), in a rural setting a five-minute drive south of town. The café is just part of a family-owned business that cultivates and collects their own mussels to steam up for customers in the café. There's also **Success Café** (104 Kapanga Rd., 07/866-7100; daily for breakfast and lunch, Thurs.–Mon. for dinner; $8–16), featuring lots of seafood, burgers, and sandwiches. Their advertising says "Try our Mussel Chowder." I did, and it's delicious.

In the name of research I also sampled the seafood tasting plate at **Pepper Tree Restaurant** (31 Kapanga Rd., 07/866-82119; daily 10 A.M.–9 P.M.; $26–36). The Pepper Tree is Coromandel's premier dining room, with a small courtyard the preferred option on a warm summer night. Along with the chowder, dishes such as the daily fish special are all very well priced.

Information

For more information on the village and areas to the north, stop by the **Coromandel Information Centre** (355 Kapanga Rd., 07/866-8598; Mon.–Fri. 9 A.M.–5 P.M., Sat.–Sun. 10 A.M.–4 P.M.), along the main road through town.

Colville

At the end of the sealed road, 30 km (19 mi) north of Coromandel, this small settlement has only one store, a restaurant, and a post office, and is the very *last* place to get supplies and petrol before heading on to the northern tip. **Green Snapper Cafe** (2314 Colville Rd., 07/866-6697; Wed.–Sun. 9 A.M.–3 P.M.; $9–16) is the local gathering spot, while the village also has a general store with petrol pumps.

North to Port Jackson

If heading to Port Jackson is what you have in mind, expect to ford several streams (generally not too deep except after heavy rains) along this coast-hugging gravel road. You'll pass stretches of beautiful coastline with enchanting bays and excellent camping spots, and wind up at the open white sands of Port Jackson beach—lots more perfect camping spots beside crystal-clear streams, plenty of driftwood for campfires, and relatively few fellow explorers. What more could you ask for? The road leads around the top of the peninsula and ends at Fletcher Bay.

On a small hilltop farm, **Fletcher Bay Backpackers** (07/866-6712, www.fletcherbay.co.nz, camping $16 per person, dorm beds $21), at the northern tip of the peninsula, is one of the remotest accommodations in the country. It's easy to spend a few days here—hiking the Coromandel Track, fishing, boating, swimming, or diving. The alternative is to camp out. The DOC administers four camping areas in the vicinity of Fletcher Bay—at Fantail Bay, Port Jackson, Stony Bay, and Waikawau Bay. All have freshwater streams, but no toilets.

Coromandel Track

This seven-km (four-mi) track, part of the New Zealand Walkway network, wanders within Cape Colville Farm Park in the far northern tip of the peninsula, from Fletcher Bay to Stony Bay. It takes about 2.5 hours each way. On this rather isolated track you traverse beach, open farmland, and bush, and are rewarded with fabulous coastal scenery. The track follows an easy grade for the most part, with only one short, steep section (marked with red disks) near the center. The small, sandy beach at Poley Bay (where a stream runs out to sea) may tempt you in for a swim, but resist the urge. Many submerged rocks lie dangerously close to the surface, and you'll find safer swimming at the end of the track. Also avoid drinking from this stream—the water is bad. Farther along, the track wanders through scrub, with the Moehau Range dominating the skyline to the west. Behind Stony Bay beach, Stony Bay and Doctors Creeks merge to form a large lagoon—a good swimming hole. A separate track leads from Stony Bay to the summit of Moehau (892 m/2,927 mi) and down the other side; allow six hours one-way. The views are worth the long, hard climb, and if you're lucky you may see one of the "fairies" that Maori legends claim inhabit this area. Campsites and freshwater streams are at both ends of the track, and Fletcher Bay has toilets.

ACROSS THE COROMANDEL PENINSULA

Many roads cross the Coromandel Peninsula. The main sealed road is **Highway 25A,** which begins south of Thames at Kopu and ends 24 km (15 mi) north of Whangamata. Farther north, drivers taking the winding unsealed Tapu Hill route from Tapu to Coroglen are rewarded with views of lush valleys, clear streams, giant tree ferns, and near the top of the range, the 2,500-year-old "Square Kauri."

From the north end of the peninsula, you have two choices. The 309 Road cuts across the peninsula, while Highway 25, the route up the coast from Thames, continues beyond Coromandel as a rough unpaved road, following a remote peninsula to Kuaotunu and on to Whitianga. Allow at least one hour for these 46 km (29 mi).

309 Road

The most interesting route across the peninsula is the 32-km-long (20-mi) unsealed 309 Road between Coromandel and Highway 25 four km (2.5 mi) southwest of Whitianga (allow at least 40 minutes to an hour depending on your familiarity with curvy gravel roads); take plenty of film to capture natural bush panoramas. The first worthwhile stop is **The Waterworks** (07/866-7191; Nov.–Apr. daily 9 A.M.–6 P.M., May–Oct. daily 10 A.M.–4 P.M.; adult $20, senior and child $15), where inventive owner Chris Ogilvie has created a number of interesting water-powered machines that are dotted around his garden. At the 7.5-km (five-mi) mark, a short trail leads to **Waiau Falls,** where sparkling water cascades over a rocky ledge surrounded by dense greenery. Just 500 meters (about 0.5 mi) farther east is a grove of kauri trees that escaped logging. They are reached by a short 10-minute (each way) trail.

WHITIANGA

Whitianga (pop. 3,800), 44 km (27 mi) southeast of Coromandel and 84 km (52 mi) northeast of Thames, is the largest town on magnificent **Mercury Bay,** on the east coast of the Coromandel Peninsula. With a sheltered harbor and long, sandy **Buffalo Beach,**

© ANDREW HEMPSTEAD

Many waterfalls can be seen along the 309 Road.

Whitianga is a popular holiday resort with countless holiday homes populated by a fairly large retirement community; in summer they're inundated with families on vacation. It's also a base for big-game fishing and scuba diving, and for a short time was on the world map as the home base of the small Mercury Bay Boating Club, which Michael Fay used when he challenged the America's Cup in 1988.

Sights and Recreation

From downtown, **Whitianga Ferry** (07/866-5472; adult $5, child $3 round-trip) runs across the Narrows (7:30 A.M.–noon and 1–6:30 P.M.) to tranquil **Ferry Landing** (original site of Whitianga), several scenic reserves featuring ocean views and sandy beaches, and the hamlet of Cooks Beach.

Near the Whitianga side of the ferry, **Mercury Bay Museum** (11 The Esplanade, 07/866-0730; daily 10 A.M.–4 P.M.; adult $5, child $0.50) is filled with photos and items from the days of the earliest pioneers. Highlights

include relics from the HMS *Buffalo,* which was wrecked nearby in 1840, and the gigantic jaws of a white pointer shark that was estimated to weigh 1,300 kg (2,860 pounds).

Accommodations

Whitianga's many motels, backpacker lodges, and holiday parks provide quite a choice in accommodation. Rates given below are for January; outside of this month, expect discounted rates. Generally, it is the more expensive places that offer the larger discounts.

A good choice for budget travelers is **Cats Pajamas** (12 Albert St., 07/866-4663, www.catspajamas.co.nz, dorm beds $25, doubles $54–70), across the road from the beach on the north side of downtown, with modern facilities, a spa pool, and bike rentals. Another good choice is **On the Beach Backpackers Lodge** (46 Buffalo Beach Rd., 07/866-5380, www.coromandelbackpackers.com, dorm beds $25, $35 s, $54–90 d). The Spanish-style building faces a large reserve, the

© ANDREW HEMPSTEAD

Whitianga oceanfront

beach, and the bay, and the enthusiastic owners offer guests the free use of kayaks, surfboards, and body boards, and have bikes for rent.

In the heart of downtown, the ◖ **Whitianga Marina Hotel** (1 Blacksmith Lane, 07/866-5818, www.whitiangahotel.co.nz, daily 11 A.M.–9 P.M.; $60–90 s or d) is an old hotel that has a renovated downstairs bar and a trendy restaurant that opens to the marina. The upstairs guest rooms remain in their original state, but are a good value at $60 for a double with shared bathroom to $90 for an en suite with TV.

Marina Park Apartments (84 Albert St., 07/866-0599 or 0800/743-784, www.marinapark.co.nz, summer $180–295 s or d) is a modern three-story complex with a swimming pool. Each spacious room has a full kitchen with stainless steel appliances, laundry facilities, one or more separate bedrooms, and a balcony or patio with harbor views.

North around the bay is the upscale **Mercury Bay Beachfront Resort** (113 Buffalo Beach Rd., 07/866-5637, www.beachfrontresort.co.nz, $250–350 s or d). Each of the eight units has either a balcony or patio overlooking a garden—the only thing separating the resort from the beach.

Food

As a seaside resort town, Whitianga has plenty of choices when it comes to casual cafés and restaurants, but my favorite is **Eggsentric** (1049 Purangi Rd., Flaxmill Bay, 07/866-0307; daily 9 A.M.–9 P.M.), which can be reached via the Whitianga Ferry and then a short walk (or you can call for a pickup). Set in landscaped gardens dotted with wood sculptures, the restaurant and food are excellent. Breakfast choices range from corn hotcakes to crayfish; in the evening, the seafood platter ($50 for one person, $95 for two) allows a chance to sample seven local delicacies from the ocean.

For meat pies with a difference, head to **Oliver's Bakery** (74 Alberta St., 07/866-0069; daily 5 A.M.–3 P.M.), back in town, and order a smoked kahawai (fish) or creamy mussel.

Right on the water, **❰ Salt** (1 Blacksmith Lane, 07/866-5818; daily 10 A.M.–9 P.M.; $35–39) has more tables outside under palm trees than it does inside. Regardless of where you are seated the food is good, with delicious seafood stew a warm-up for a well-presented steak, veal, or chicken main.

Information

At **Whitianga Visitor Information Centre** (66 Albert St., 07/866-5555, www.whitianga. co.nz, Mon.–Fri. 9 A.M.–5 P.M., Sat.–Sun. 9 A.M.–4 P.M.), ask to see the photo album that tells the story about the friendly sea lion who fell in love with Clara, a local cow, back in the 1990s. The center also has public Internet access.

HAHEI AND VICINITY

Hahei, 30 km (19 mi) south of Whitianga, is best known for its sheltered soft pink beach (caused by crushed shells mixed in with the sand) and dramatic headlands with two *pa* sites at the southern end. Beyond the *pa* lie two blowholes, magnificent at high tide in stormy weather. At the northern end of Hahei Beach (signposted along Grange Rd.), a two-km/one-mi (45-minute) one-way walk descends to **Cathedral Cove,** where you can walk through a huge sea cavern, and a magnificent white sandy beach. The **Hahei Explorer** (07/866-3910, adult $70, child $40) is an inflatable boat that cruises around local waters to Cathedral Cove, Hot Water Beach, or snorkeling spots. **Cathedral Cove Sea Kayaking** (07/866-3877) charges $95 for a three-hour paddle or $150 for a full day on the water.

❰ Hot Water Beach

This unassuming stretch of sand nine km (5.6 mi) south of Hahei off Hahei Beach Road hides another of New Zealand's many and varied natural attractions. And best of all, this one is

Cathedral Cove

free. Flooded at high tide, this area is accessible for about three hours either side of low tide, when locals and visitors alike take baths in the warm spring water that seeps up through the sand. Allow about 15 minutes to dig a hole in the sand below the high-tide mark (spades can be rented from the adjacent café), and voilê, your own private hot pool! The deeper you dig, the warmer the water.

On the way back from Hot Water Beach to Hahei, look for a sign to the left marking **Kauri Grove Walk.** This walk leads down through exotic tree ferns and native bush to a small stream, and then parallels the stream, which descends in a series of small waterfalls. Birdsong, the buzz of cicadas, and the whistling stream add to the all-around beauty. The track eventually crosses the stream and climbs into a young kauri forest. The first loop takes about 90 minutes round-trip, the track that leads to the coast is 2.5 hours one-way, and the one to the coast and on to Sailor's Bay is three hours one-way.

Accommodations and Food

The small village of Hahei has a choice of accommodations, a general store, and a small café. Behind the store is **Tatahi Lodge** (19 Grange Rd., 07/866-3992, www.tatahilodge.co.nz), which offers modern backpacker rooms and a small number of self-contained units. Bikes are available for rent, guests have free use of adjacent tennis courts, and the hosts can arrange all local activities. The backpacker section is as good as you'll find anywhere in the country (dorm beds $29, $86 d). Across the courtyard are private rooms ($220 s or d) and self-contained units, with separate bedrooms and furnished in a casual yet elegant "beachy" style ($250).

The Church (87 Hahei Beach Rd., 07/866-3533, www.thechurchhahei.co.nz, $135–230 s or d) offers accommodation in cottages set among wonderful gardens and surrounded by native bush. As the name suggests, a church is on the property—transformed from a

small-town place of worship to **The Church** (07/866-3797; daily from 5:30 P.M.; $29–36), an upscale restaurant that features well-presented dishes of local game and produce.

On the hill above town (toward Cathedral Cove) is **Spellbound** (77 Grange Rd., 07/866-3543, www.spellboundhahei.co.nz, $150–165 s, $180–195 d). Each of the three comfortable rooms in this modern bed-and-breakfast enjoys ocean views and has its own bathroom. A continental breakfast is served on an outdoor deck, and dinner is available at an extra cost.

TAIRUA AND PAUANUI

Popular with vacationers, particularly in summer, the twin towns of Tairua and Pauanui are separated by a narrow tidal waterway 57 km (35 mi) south of Whitianga. Tairua, on Highway 25, is the older, more established town. Reached by ferry ($5 round-trip) or road (from Hwy. 25 south of Tairua), Pauanui is a modern subdivision punctuated by artificial canals. Just north of Tairua, keep your eyes peeled for **Twin Kauri Scenic Reserve**—two stunning kauri trees standing side by side right next to the road (easily missed if you're coming from the north—look for the small pullout).

Accommodations

Motels in Tairua are generally more expensive than elsewhere on the peninsula, but this reflects the quality more than anything else. For the atmosphere of a tropical island, consider spending the night at **Pacific Harbour Lodge** (223 Main Rd., 07/864-8581, www.pacificharbour.co.nz, $179–269 s or d), complete with palm trees and shell-lined paths as well as tastefully decorated freestanding cottages. Well worth the extra money for the additional living space are the King Luxury Chalets. Amenities include a restaurant, business center, and day spa.

Across the water, **Puka Park Resort** (Mount Ave., Pauanui, 07/864-8088, www.pukapark.co.nz, from $350 s or d) is one of the peninsula's most appealing resorts. Set among 10 hectares (25 acres) of native bush, the 47 freestanding chalets offer the utmost in luxury, with guests taking advantage of a large outdoor pool complex, café, restaurant, and bar. In relation to comparable resorts in North America and Europe (where most guests are from), the rates at Puka Park are very reasonable; packages advertised on the resort website make a stay even more so.

SOUTH FROM TAIRUA
Opoutere

From Tairua, continue down Highway 25 south from the junction of Highway 25 and Highway 25A 11 km (6.8 mi) to Keenan's Corner, from where it's four km (2.5 mi) to the relaxed seaside village of Opoutere. **YHA Opoutere** (389 Opoutere Rd., 07/865-9072, www.yha.co.nz, dorm beds $27, $84 d) is ideally situated for hiking and beachcombing. Backed by native bush and edging a tidal estuary, this converted schoolhouse has the added bonus of being within a few minutes' walk of Opoutere Beach. The nearest shop is four km (2.5 mi) away, but the hostel shop sells a wide range of supplies, including vegetarian and health foods.

Whangamata

This popular holiday resort and retirement community of 3,600 lies at the southern end of a magnificent beach 38 km (24 mi) south of Tairua and 60 km (37 mi) east of Thames. Its great surf is popular with both serious surfers and swimmers who enjoy large waves. Whangamata (faan-ga-mata) also boasts good surf fishing. For dive and fishing charter information, continue along Port Road to the wharf, where there's an information board. **Ocean Beach,** reached via Ocean Road from the highway, is a long stretch of golden sand with offshore bush-covered islands—worth a drive out there whether you're going to catch it on film, work on your tan, or plunge into the Pacific.

Brenton Lodge (2 Brenton Pl., 07/865-8400; www.brentonlodge.co.nz, $370 s, $390 d) takes in the panorama of Whangamata and the ocean from afar. Guests stay in the main house or two garden cottages, but all enjoy fresh flowers, fresh fruit, and muffins on arrival. The grounds hold a large pool and well-tended gardens set around mature trees. Rates include a choice of cooked breakfasts.

Waihi and Waihi Beach

These two towns are crowded with vacationers and tourists in summer, but Waihi, inland at the junction of Highways 2 and 25, also has a colorful gold-mining history, with the rich Martha Mine still operating. **Waihi Gold Mining Museum** (54 Kenny St., 07/863-8386; Thurs.–Fri. 10 A.M.–3 P.M., Sat.–Sun. noon–3 P.M.; adult $5, child $3) has a model of the mine and lots of related relics.

Waihi Beach, 11 km (seven mi) east of Waihi, is considered one of the safest beaches along the coast—it's patrolled in summer and on holidays by local lifesaving club members. **Waihi Beach Top 10 Holiday Resort** (15 Beach Rd., 07/863-5504, www.waihibeach.com, campsites $36, cabins and motel rooms $85–150 s or d) offers communal facilities, TV and game rooms, and a general store.

From Waihi, it's 35 km (22 mi) south to Tauranga, with Highway 2 paralleling Tauranga Harbour for much of the way. Tauranga and the surrounding areas are part of the Bay of Plenty.

HIGHWAY 2 WEST FROM WAIHI

From Waihi, Highway 2 cuts back across the southern end of the Coromandel Peninsula. The first stretch of this route, to Paeroa, is quite scenic, particularly toward the Paeroa end where the highway parallels Karangahake Gorge (part of the Ohinemuri Goldfield, opened in 1875) and River, edged by tall pampas grass and luxuriant tree ferns. Stop at **Karangahake Reserve** to stroll the 4.5-km (three-mi) **Karangahake Gorge Historic Walkway;** do the loop track or continue to Owharoa Falls. The track meanders along the river, passing old bridges, abandoned mining equipment and relics, and mining shafts (stay on the track)—a walk back in time. The walkway is signposted from the highway at each end—at the Waihi end, pull off to take a short amble down through another small, incredibly lush, scenic reserve to impressive **Owharoa Falls.** Several craft shops are signposted off the highway.

Paeroa

At the western end of Karangahake Gorge, Paeroa (pop. 4,000) grew as an inland port and is now a bustling rural service center at the junction of Highways 2 and 26, 38 km (24 mi) west of Waihi and 32 km (20 mi) south of Thames. The local claim to fame is Lemon and Paeroa, a soft drink that combined local mineral water and lemon. Bottled at a plant on the main street and cherished countrywide, it's no longer produced. A seven-meter-high (23-ft) L&P bottle at the southern end of town is all that's left of the legend. Of lesser fame but more interest is **Paeroa Historical Maritime Park,** three km (two mi) northwest of downtown along Highway 2. At the site of the original port, the park is the scene of an ongoing restoration project that includes the 1897 paddlesteamer *Kopu,* rescued from a silt-laden grave in the riverbed.

Bay of Plenty

Captain Cook first sailed these shores in 1769; on finding several friendly and prosperous Maori villages along the coast he was able to restock badly needed provisions, prompting him to name the area the Bay of Plenty. But the bay's history long predates Cook. According to Maori legends, nine of the original 22 emigrant canoes from Hawaiiki landed in this area, and it became home for some of the strongest and most powerful Maori tribes. You can view the remains of many *pa* along its shores. But the golden sand and crystal-clear waters are the primary attractions for visitors—including thousands of Kiwis.

TAURANGA

The city and port of Tauranga (Sheltered Anchorage) is 220 km (137 mi) southeast of Auckland and 88 km (55 mi) north of Rotorua. With a population of 110,000, it lies along a section of the large and sprawling Tauranga Harbour. Tauranga is a good place to go when you're tired of being on the road. Lots of beautiful parks and no major attractions give you the

excuse to lie back and do nothing. However, if you plan to do some white-water rafting during your stay in the North Island, look into the several rafting companies based in Tauranga. Unrivaled excitement on some of the North Island's most exhilarating rivers awaits the adventurous spirit, and Tauranga is a good place to investigate a variety of trips.

Sights and Recreation

The main shopping drag in Tauranga is **The Strand,** but you can escape the hustle and bustle of the commercial center by strolling through the **Strand Gardens** on the eastern side of the street. For an enjoyable one-hour walk back a hundred years, continue to the northern end of The Strand, where the intricately carved Maori war canoe *Te Awanui* is on display, and then follow the path up to the complex earthworks of **Monmouth Redoubt.** This area, commonly called "The Camp," was the site of the original 1864 military settlement that overlooked the bay. The oval-shaped

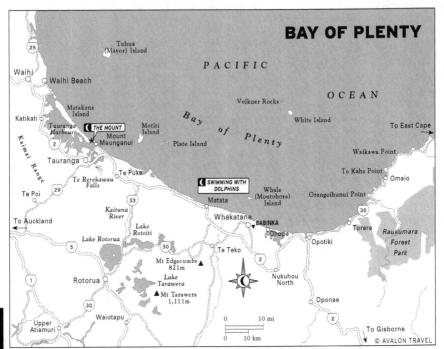

BAY OF PLENTY

PACIFIC

OCEAN

Tuhua
(Mayor) Island

Waihi

Waihi Beach

Katikati

Matakana
Island

Tauranga
Harbour

THE MOUNT

Mount
Maunganui

Tauranga

Motiti
Island

Plate Island

Volkner Rocks

White Island

Bay of Plenty

To East Cape

Waikawa Point

Te Kaha Point

Omaio

Kaimai Range

Te Puke

Te Rerekawau
Falls

Te Poi

29

33

Kaituna
River

Matata

**SWIMMING WITH
DOLPHINS**

Whale
(Moutohora)
Island

Orangoihunui Point

Whakatane

BABINKA

Ohope

Opotiki

Torere

35

Raukumara
Forest
Park

To Auckland

5

Lake
Rotorua

Lake
Rotoiti

30

Te Teko

2

Nukuhou
North

Opotiki

1

Rotorua

Mt Edgecumbe
821m

Lake
Tarawera

Mt Tarawera
1,111m

Oponae

Upper
Atiamuri

30

Waiotapu

0   10 mi

0   10 km

2

To Gisborne

© AVALON TRAVEL

Robbins Park, on the knoll between the redoubt and the cemetery, has a Begonia House (open daily) and rose gardens within its grounds. For fairly graphic descriptions of Tauranga's past, check out the gravestones in the **Military Cemetery** on Cliff Road—some have quite a story to tell.

Off Cliff Road, **The Elms** (Mission St., 07/577-9772; Wed., Sat.–Sun. 2–4 P.M.; adult $5) was the original mission house built between 1838 and 1847 by the missionary Reverend Brown. The Elms is privately owned, but the grounds are open to the public dawn to dusk and the house itself is open for a couple of hours three afternoons a week.

The bores at Tauranga are the source of internationally known Fernland Sparkling Mineral Water, but if you'd rather immerse yourself in it than drink it, head for **Fernland Spa** (250 Cambridge Rd., Te Reti, 07/578-3081; daily

8:30 A.M.–10 P.M.; adult $8, senior $6, child $5). Entry to the private pools is $11 per 30 minutes. The water (38–40°C/100–104°F) is pumped daily from 200 meters (660 ft) beneath the ground into the main public pool and eight large private pools. From downtown (about six km/3.7 mi from the post office) follow Cameron Street to 11th Avenue and turn right; 11th becomes Waihi Road. Continue along Waihi, then turn left onto Cambridge Road.

At the bottom of a fairly steep track through native bush you'll find **Te Rerekawau Falls**— actually three beautiful waterfalls (formerly called Kaiate Falls), the third plummeting into a very deep, bush-fringed pool and popular (icy-cold!) swimming hole. It's a great place for photographers in search of slow-speed water shots. You'll need a car to get to these falls, but keep all valuables locked out of sight or with you. Take Highway 2 out of Tauranga

---

TUHUA (MAYOR) ISLAND

If you're looking for somewhere to get away from just about everyone, 1,280-hectare (3,160-acre) Tuhua Island—40 km (25 mi) offshore from Tauranga—is the place for you. Privately owned but managed by a trust, Tuhua is the remnant of an ancient volcano that last erupted approximately 6,000 years ago. It's been dormant ever since and is a quiet place, covered in native forest and inhabited by abundant birdlife such as bellbird, *tui*, *kaka*, kingfisher, and the recently reintroduced North Island robin. The surrounding crystal-clear waters are filled with marinelife, and a trail leads up and over the eroded volcanic rim to two colorful lakes within the ancient crater.

GETTING TO THE ISLAND

Access to Tuhua is by charter boat from Tauranga. **Tauranga Marine Charters** (07/552-6283, www.taurangamarinecharters.co.nz) and **Blue Ocean Charters** (07/554-3072, www.blueoceancharters.co.nz) provide island transfers out of both Tauranga and Mount Maunganui on demand. Expect to pay about $130 per person round-trip. You also pay a $5-per-person landing fee, and as the island is predator-free, visitors must unpack their day pack in the presence of a caretaker upon arrival.

---

toward Mount Maunganui, but turn right toward Welcome Bay before crossing the harbor. Continue along Welcome Bay Road, and just after the bay turn right on Waitao Road—the falls are signposted from here.

Entertainment

The Strand is lined with bars and restaurants with lots of outdoor tables—the perfect place to while away an hour or two on a warm afternoon or evening. The always lively **Za Bar** (53 The Strand, 07/579-9236) is popular for

its welcoming staff and wide selection of food and drink. Along similar lines, **Syndicate** (107 The Strand, 07/578-3543) is a big, stylish space with lots of polished wood and a menu that is a notch above regular pub food.

Accommodations and Camping

YHA Tauranga (171 Elizabeth St., 07/578-5064, www.yha.co.nz, dorm beds $26, $68–84 s or d) provides budget accommodation within walking distance of downtown. It has the usual communal facilities, nearby waterside walking tracks, a variety of outdoor games, and a barbecue.

Located 3.5 km (two mi) from downtown, **Bell Lodge** (39 Bell St., 07/578-6344, dorm beds $28–33, $65 s or d, motel room $95 s or d) has excellent budget accommodations—heated bunkrooms—plus a fully equipped communal kitchen, a spacious dining room and TV area, a guest lounge, and a coin-op laundry.

Strand Motel (27 The Strand, 07/578-5807, www.strandmotel.co.nz, $85 s or d) is an old motel, but it's centrally located and a good value. It's within easy walking distance of everything, each unit has a kitchen, and the four upstairs rooms enjoy water views.

Harbour View Motel (7 Fifth Ave., 07/578-8621, www.harbourviewmotel.co.nz, $115–145 s or d) is slightly older than the Strand Motel, but it's right on the water in a quiet location 800 meters (0.5 mi) south of downtown. Each room has a kitchen and tea- and coffee-making facilities.

Many motels can be found on or near Cameron Street, which runs the length of the peninsula upon which Tauranga lies. One of the best of these is **Academy Motor Inn** (734 Cameron St. at 15th Ave., 07/578-9103 or 0800/782-9222, www.academymotorinn.co.nz, $110–210 s or d), with 20 self-contained units featuring many nice touches, such as hair dryers. The complex includes a swimming pool, spa pool, and barbecue area.

HOLIDAY PARKS

Silver Birch Holiday Park (101 Turret Rd., 07/578-4603, www.silverbirch.co.nz, camping $38, cabins $90–130 s or d) enjoys a quiet waterfront location four km (2.5 mi) south of downtown off Highway 2 to Whakatane (Turret Rd. is an extension of 15th Ave.). Amenities include modern communal facilities, a TV and game room, a boat ramp, use of mineral swimming pools, and a general store.

If being in town isn't a priority, plan on camping at **Fernland Spa** (250 Cambridge Rd., Te Reti, 07/578-3081, www.fernlandspa.co.nz), where the overnight fee of $30 per site includes access to the hot springs.

Food

Cafés and restaurants line The Strand between Harrington and Wharf Streets opposite the harbor, with cobbled sidewalks complete with flowerbeds and old-fashioned lampposts creating the perfect atmosphere for outdoor dining.

On a sunny day on The Strand, it's hard to go past C **Fresh Fish Market** (1 Dive Crescent, 07/578-1789; daily from 10:30 A.M.; $10–15) for casual outdoor dining. Right on the dock at the north end of The Strand, surrounded by fishing boats, the market offers all types of fresh and cooked fish. It has a couple of tables; you can also wander along the wharf and enjoy your meal with the seagulls.

The menu—Love Me Ten-Deer (baked venison medallions), Stand by Your Lamb (roasted lamb doused in mint sauce), and more—is a giveaway that the **Horny Bull** (67 The Strand, 07/578-8741; Mon.–Fri. from 11 A.M., Sat.–Sun. from 9 A.M. for lunch and dinner; $25–36) doesn't take itself too seriously. But the food is good and with most mains under $30, it's a good place for a meal.

Like the surrounding eateries, **Naked Grape** (97 The Strand, 07/579-5555; Mon.–Sat. 7:30 A.M.–midnight, Sun. 8 A.M.–4 P.M.; $26–34) maximizes its location with lots of outdoor

tables overlooking the water. Expect to pay $14 for a stack of pancakes topped with maple-glazed bananas and $30 for fish of the day at dinner.

For seafood without the seagulls, it's hard to beat **Harbourside** (The Strand, 07/571-0520; daily 11:30 A.M.–9:30 P.M.; $24–38). Built over the water as a yacht club in 1933, the original structure has been converted to a fine restaurant, losing none of its nautical charm along the way. Most tables enjoy harbor views, but the very best sit along a covered verandah. In addition to lots of seafood (including the delicious Harbourside Bouillabasse), the menu features a variety of light pastas and salads.

Information and Services

The first place to head for information on Tauranga and Mount Maunganui is the **Tauranga Visitor Centre** (one block north of The Strand at 95 Willow St., 07/577-6234, www.bayofplentynz.com, Mon.–Fri. 7 A.M.–5:30 P.M., Sat.–Sun. 8 A.M.–4 P.M.). Part of the bus depot, it has brochures and tourist newspapers, and also gives out information on Tuhua Island. The **Automobile Association** has an office at the corner of Devonport Road and 1st Avenue (07/578-2222).

The post office is at 17 Grey Street. You can reach **Tauranga Hospital** on Cameron Road at 07/579-8000.

Getting There and Around

If you're short on time, **Air New Zealand** (07/577-7300 or 0800/737-300, www.airnewzealand.com) has direct flights to Tauranga from Auckland and Wellington. The airport is on the Mount Maunganui side of the city, off Hewletts Road. **Tauranga Mount Taxis** (07/578-6086, $12 per person) has a door-to-door shuttle to Tauranga and Mount Maunganui from the airport. **Intercity** (www.intercity.co.nz) coaches connect Tauranga with Auckland, Thames, Hamilton, Rotorua, Whakatane, Opotiki, and Gisborne. The depot is the **Tauranga Visitor Centre** (95 Willow St., 07/578-8103).

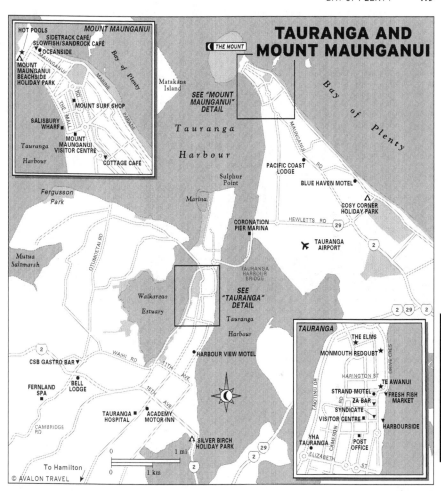

Baybus (0800/422-928) runs a local bus service through all the suburbs and to Mount Maunganui; $2.60 per sector, or ride all day for $7.30. Local cab companies include **Tauranga Mount Taxis** (07/578-6086) and **Citicabs** (07/577-0999).

MOUNT MAUNGANUI

Known for its wonderful surf beach and mellow vacation atmosphere, Mount Maunganui (pop. 17,000) sprawls across a low peninsula

just a five-minute drive from Tauranga. Separated from that much larger city by a tidal estuary (but linked by a bridge), "the Mount," as it's usually known, is made up of row upon row of holiday homes. The real estate boom of the last decade has seen many of the older "baches" be replaced with million-dollar homes and shiny new condos, especially at the north end, where, lo and behold, there's a perfectly symmetrical volcano surrounded by water on three sides.

© ANDREW HEMPSTEAD

Walkers and sheep mix on the trails around Mount Maunganui.

⟨ The Mount

Just by looking at its classically conical shape you can see how the Mount made an impressive Maori *pa* in the 18th and 19th centuries (you can still see the old fortifications, particularly on the southeastern side, facing town). Several walking tracks lead to the top of this 234-meter (770-ft) peak (allow 50 minutes to reach the summit), where your effort is rewarded with a magnificent 360-degree panoramic view. An easier track circles the base of the mountain; it takes about an hour to complete the circular route.

At the foot of the volcano, unique **hot saltwater pools** (9 Adams Ave., 07/575-0868; Mon.–Sat. 6 A.M.–10 P.M., Sun. 8 A.M.–10 P.M.; adult $10.20, senior $7.70, child $5.40) are the only ones of their kind in the Southern Hemisphere. The salt water comes from a 40-meter-deep (130-ft-deep) bore, and when the water is first brought up from underground it's a sizzling 45°C (113°F). The water is cooled to a still-hot 39°C (102°F) before being pumped into the large main pool and several (hotter) smaller pools; this is a great place to soothe aching muscles and tired feet.

Beaches

The most popular beach in this area is **Mount Maunganui Beach,** directly opposite the concentration of restaurants at the north end of Marine Parade. This wide stretch of sand offers safe swimming and the distinctive volcano as a backdrop. Tiny **Moturiki Island** is linked to the mainland by a sandbar along this stretch of sand and is laced with walking tracks. The golden sands and sparkling surf stretch for almost 16 km (10 mi) southeast from this point, and can be reached from Marine Parade on the eastern side of Mount Maunganui and from Papamoa Beach. Additionally, small, sheltered harbor beaches run along Pilot Bay, ending at Salisbury Wharf on the western side of town.

Experienced surfers will tell you there are better breaks elsewhere, but the sandy bottom

© ANDREW HEMPSTEAD

The beaches at Mount Maunganui are among the country's best.

and rolling waves make the Mount one of the most popular surf spots in the country. **Mount Surf Shop** (96 Maunganui Rd., 07/575-9133; daily 9 A.M.–5 P.M.) rents surfboards ($40 per day) and wet suits ($25).

Accommodations and Camping

Accommodation around the Mount is relatively expensive, especially in January, when reservations are needed far in advance.

◖ Pacific Coast Lodge (432 Maunganui Rd., 07/574-9601 or 0800/666-622, www.pacificcoastlodge.co.nz, dorm beds $26–30, $72–83 s or d) is a large, modern, professionally operated backpacker lodge along the main road into town and a few blocks from the beach. All facilities are excellent, including a large kitchen and dining area, a TV room, a laundry, and a courtyard. The double rooms are on a different level from the dorms and share their own bathrooms.

One of the cheapest motels is the **Blue Haven Motel** (10 Tweed St., 07/575-6508,

www.bluehaven.co.nz, $85–100 s, $110–125 d). A flat 10-minute walk from the beach, the motel has nine units, each featuring a full kitchen. Out front is a grassed picnic area with a barbecue for guest use.

It's impossible to miss the "twin towers" rising high above the beach. They are part of **Oceanside** (1 Maunganui Rd., 07/575-5371, www.oceanside.co.nz, $210–550), with two heated outdoor pools, a fitness room, a sauna, and easy access to the downstairs cafés lining Marine Parade. The least expensive rooms don't have water views, but high up in the towers are oversized two-bedroom apartments with big balconies and even bigger views.

Mount Maunganui Beachside Holiday Park (1 Adams Ave., 07/575-4471, www.mount-beachside.co.nz, campsites $55, cabins $130 s or d) is an old-fashioned campground, with sites around the hot-water pools at the base of the Mount and on both ocean and harbor beaches.

Cosy Corner Holiday Park, four km (2.5

mi) east of the Mount (40 Ocean Beach Rd., Omanu, 07/575-5899, www.cosycorner.co.nz, campsites $40, cabins $70–140 s or d) has a wonderful location across the road from the beach, and a big solar-heated pool if you get tired of salt water.

Food

The most popular cafés and restaurants are those under "the Towers" at the north end of Marine Parade, but be forewarned—finding an empty table is not easy, especially on weekends. The first to open is **Sidetrack Café** (Marine Pde., 07/575-2145; daily 6:30 A.M.–4 P.M.; lunches $10–19), with strong coffee and delicious vanilla pancakes with roast banana—a good start to the day.

Slow food—as opposed to "fast food"—is a growing worldwide movement that has found its way to Mount Maunganui in the form of **Slowfish** (Marine Pde., 07/574-2949; daily 7 A.M.–4 P.M.; $12–20). Everything is healthy and made in-house, with ingredients locally sourced; organic ingredients are used wherever possible. The result? A mouthwatering eggs Florentine, fish cakes with chili jam, and poached chicken on a bed of organic greens.

The usual array of cafés, bakeries, and inexpensive Asian restaurants are scattered along Maunganui Road. For homemade baked goods to enjoy inside or outside in the sunshine, try **Cottage Cafe** (373 Maunganui Rd., 07/575-3733; daily 8:30 A.M.–4 P.M.; lunches $8–15). Don't be put off by the unappealing decor.

Information and Services

All you really need to know is where the beach is, but for information on local accommodations, head to **Mount Maunganui Visitor Centre** (Salisbury Ave., 07/575-5099; Mon.–Fri. 9 A.M.–5 P.M., weekends in summer only).

The post office is at the back of an arcade, one shop from the BNZ Bank on the main street before you reach the Mount. **Mount Medical Centre** is at 257 Maunganui Road (07/575-3073).

Tauranga to the East Cape

TE PUKE

The largest town between Tauranga/Mount Maunganui and Whakatane is Te Puke (pop. 6,800), 20 km (12 mi) from Tauranga along Highway 2. The town, nestled in the middle of a large kiwifruit growing area, calls itself the "Kiwifruit Capital of the World," and with over 90 percent of the country's kiwifruit coming for the region, no one disputes the claim.

Sights and Recreation

Kiwi 360 (82 Young Rd., 07/573-6340; daily 9 A.M.–5 P.M.; adult $20, senior $18, child $6), six km (four mi) through town to the east, is a horticultural theme park in a working orchard. Admission to the park includes a ride on a kiwifruit-shaped trailer through the orchard, a tour of the packaging plant, and fruit-tasting and wine-tasting. The Kiwi 360 Café (daily 10 A.M.–3 P.M.) offers a lot of outdoor seating and a kiwifruit-themed menu that includes kiwifruit juice and wine.

WHAKATANE

Go to Whakatane (fah-kah-tah-nee), population 19,000, around the Bay of Plenty 100 km (62 mi) southeast of Tauranga, to enjoy the sunshine, the beaches, and the relaxed atmosphere. The best-known surf beach, **Ohope Beach,** six km (3.7 mi) east from Whakatane, attracts surfers and fishermen year-round, holidaymakers by the hordes in summer, and hikers in search of great coastal views.

You'll know you're in kiwifruit country when you see this roadside attraction.

Whakatane Museum and Gallery

Reopened in March 2012 after extensive redevelopment, this museum (55 Boon St., 07/307-9805; Mon.–Fri. 10 A.M.–4:30 P.M., Sat.–Sun. 11 A.M.–3 P.M.; donation) is filled with an interesting collection of Maori artifacts and displays detailing their culture and lifestyle. It also has a large collection of historical photos, a New Zealand book collection, and exhibits on European settlement.

Another interesting place well worth a visit is **Tauwhare Pa,** which is beside the highway from Ohope to Opotiki (just past the harbor). Interpretive boards along a short walkway explain how the reserve may have appeared and operated in A.D. 1700 (when most Bay of Plenty *pa* were built).

Hiking

Whakatane and the surrounding area have a reputation for very enjoyable local walkways, scenic reserves, and an island wildlife sanctuary. Ask at

the information center for the helpful (and free) handouts on **Kohi Point Walkway, Whakatane Town Centre Walk, Ohope Bush Walk** (which allows hikers to walk through beautiful bush scenery from Ohope Beach to Whakatane via Ohope and Mokorua Scenic Reserves), **Lathams Hill Track, Matata Walking Track,** and **Matata Lagoon Walk** (you can see fantastic birdlife from an observation platform). **Pine Bush Scenic Reserve** allows people with disabilities to enjoy a small remnant of *kahikatea* forest and plenty of birdlife via a wheelchair walkway.

🌊 Swimming with Dolphins

Dolphins are among the most loved of all marine mammals, and you shouldn't miss the opportunity to frolic in the open ocean with these fun-loving creatures. **Diveworks** (96 The Strand, 07/308-2001, www.whaleislandtours.com, $155) offers a five- to six-hour trip out into the Bay of Plenty. During the trip you can swim with dolphins, possibly see whales (if you're lucky), and get a distant view of White Island. If you go as a spectator the cost is $105.

Accommodations and Camping

The Windsor (10 Merritt St., 07/308-8040, dorm beds $25, $66–86 s or d) is a centrally located backpacker lodge with a courtyard and barbecue.

In a prime location across from Whakatane Wharf, **White Island Rendezvous** (15 The Strand, 07/308-9500, www.whiteisland.co.nz, $140–190 s or d) is an excellent choice for an overnight stay in Whakatane. Home to White Island Tours, this accommodation comprises 27 charming units, each with a microwave and some with small kitchens. Although a little on the small side, the rooms provide good value. Wireless Internet and an on-site café add to the appeal.

On the road into town from Tauranga (just east of the Whakatane River), **37 The Landing Motel** (37 Landing Rd., 07/307-1297 or 0800/437-526, www.landingmotel.co.nz, $135–220 s or d) is a modern motel with the best rooms in town (complete with super-comfortable king beds). Most rooms have a kitchen, and there's a covered barbecue area for those balmy summer evenings.

Whakatane Holiday Park (McGarvey Rd., 07/308-8694, www.whakataneholidaypark. co.nz, camping $32, cabins from $75) offers the usual communal facilities, a TV lounge and game room, and a swimming pool, but out of town to the east, **Ohope Beach Top 10 Holiday Park** (367 Harbour Rd., 07/312-4460, www. ohopebeach.co.nz, campsites $22–23 per person, cabins from $145 s or d) is in a better location for beach lovers.

If you're going on toward Rotorua (or even if you're not), you may enjoy staying at **Awakeri Hot Springs** (07/304-9117, www.awakerisprings.co.nz, campsites $32, cabins $70 s or d, motel rooms $95). About 16 km (10 mi) from Whakatane on Highway 30, it has the usual holiday park facilities, with the added plus of warm mineral swim baths and hot mineral spa pools.

Food

Kick-start your day down along the waterfront at **PeeJay's Coffee House** (15 The Strand, 07/308-9588; daily 6:30 A.M.–2 P.M.; lunches $8–17). The base for White Island Tours, this café has a great little sunny deck off to one side. The food is surprisingly creative, with most breakfasts and lunches under $15. **The Bean** (72 The Strand, 07/307-0494; Mon.–Sat. 8 A.M.–4 P.M., Sun. 9 A.M.–3 P.M.; lunches $8–12) is another option for a light meal and good coffee, which is roasted in-house.

Continuing along the main road through downtown is the main wharf, and a couple of good eateries right in the heart of the ocean-going action. For the best fish and chips in town, head to **Wally's on the Wharf** (2 The Strand, 07/307-1100; daily 11 A.M.–8 P.M.), with a couple of tables out on the wharf the best place to enjoy this inexpensive (under $10) meal. Next door, you'll spend more money

and more time at **Wharf Shed Restaurant** (2 The Strand, 07/308-5698; daily for lunch and dinner; $26–55), which delivers consistent seafood in a stylish waterfront setting. Most lunches are around $20 (the surf and turf burger was delicious).

C Babinka (14 Kakahoroa Dr., 07/307-0009; daily 10 A.M.–2 P.M. and 5:30–9 P.M.; $22–32) is in a distinctive blue building within a shopping-mall parking lot. But don't be put off by the location—the menu is filled with modern interpretations of classic Asian dishes, with lots of curries and seafood blackboard specials under $30.

Practicalities

Whakatane Visitor Centre (corner Kakahoroa Dr. and Quay St., 07/308-6058 or 0800/942-528, www.whakatane.com, Mon.–Fri. 8:30 A.M.–6 P.M., summer also Sat.–Sun. 9 A.M.–5 P.M.) is a sweepingly modern building along the waterfront.

Whakatane Airport is on Aerodrome Road, 10 km (six mi) north of town; if you don't have your own transportation, you can take a taxi (about $20 one-way). **Air New Zealand** (07/308-8397 or 0800/737-300, www. airnewzealand.com) flies from Whakatane to Auckland and Wellington. **Intercity** (www. intercity.co.nz) connects Whakatane with Tauranga, Rotorua, and Gisborne via Opotiki. Buses stop outside the visitor center.

The only rental car agency in town is **Avis** (07/308-5636), with a few vehicles at the airport (reserve ahead). For a cab, call **Whakatane Taxi** (07/307-0388).

WHITE ISLAND

White Island lies about 50 km (31 mi) north of Whakatane, at the northern end of the Taupo-Rotorua volcanic fault line. This is an excellent active volcano to visit because of its intense thermal activity. Originally named by Captain Cook in 1769 for the shroud of steam surrounding it, the island continues to belch steam, noxious gases, and toxic fumes into the atmosphere. Occasional eruptions send up huge clouds of ash visible from the mainland, weather permitting. Geysers, fumaroles, holes of sulfuric acid, and boiling-water pools lie within the crater, best enjoyed from a safe distance—like from a helicopter!

Sulphur was mined on the island until an explosive landslide in 1914 killed all the miners and wiped out the mining settlement. Miners made several other mining attempts, but because of the unpredictable and violent nature of the island, abandoned all. Despite the lack of fresh water and the presence of toxic fumes, parts of the island are covered by *pohutukawa* trees and inhabited by quite a variety of birdlife. Gannets, red-billed gulls, and petrels seem to thrive in this strange environment and have made their breeding grounds on the island, now a private scenic reserve.

White Island Tours (15 The Strand, 07/308-9588 or 0800/733-529, www.whiteisland.co.nz, adult $185, child $120) runs to the island between one and three time daily from Whakatane Wharf. The boat trip takes about 80 minutes in a stable 20-meter (66-ft) vessel. About two hours is spent exploring the island, time enough to walk inside the crater. A light lunch is included in the tour rate. You can also visit the island by helicopter. **Vulcan Helicopters** (07/308-4188 or 0800/804-354, www.vulcanheli.co.nz, $550 for two people) offers the return transfer and a one-hour guided walk. Departures are on demand from Whakatane Airport.

BAY OF PLENTY

www.moon.com

DESTINATIONS | ACTIVITIES | BLOGS | MAPS | BOOKS

MOON.COM is ready to help plan your next trip! Filled with fresh trip ideas and strategies, author interviews, informative travel blogs, a detailed map library, and descriptions of all the Moon guidebooks, Moon.com is all you need to get out and explore the world—or even places in your own backyard. While at Moon.com, sign up for our monthly e-newsletter for updates on new releases, travel tips, and expert advice from our on-the-go Moon authors. As always, when you travel with Moon, expect an experience that is uncommon and truly unique.

KEEP UP WITH MOON ON FACEBOOK AND TWITTER
JOIN THE MOON PHOTO GROUP ON FLICKR

MAP SYMBOLS

▓▓▓	Expressway	☾	Highlight	✗	Airfield	⌕	Golf Course
⋯⋯	Primary Road	○	City/Town	✈	Airport	P	Parking Area
▬▬	Secondary Road	◉	State Capital	▲	Mountain	▰	Archaeological Site
◦ ◦ ◦	Unpaved Road	✹	National Capital	✚	Unique Natural Feature	⯭	Church
-------	Trail	★	Point of Interest			⛽	Gas Station
⋯⋯⋯	Ferry	●	Accommodation	⌇	Waterfall	◌	Glacier
~~	Railroad	▼	Restaurant/Bar	♠	Park	⌁	Mangrove
▓▓▓	Pedestrian Walkway	■	Other Location	⊡	Trailhead	▨	Reef
⟙⟙⟙	Stairs	⋏	Campground	⛷	Skiing Area	▭	Swamp

CONVERSION TABLES

°C = (°F – 32) / 1.8
°F = (°C x 1.8) + 32
1 inch = 2.54 centimeters (cm)
1 foot = 0.304 meters (m)
1 yard = 0.914 meters
1 mile = 1.6093 kilometers (km)
1 km = 0.6214 miles
1 fathom = 1.8288 m
1 chain = 20.1168 m
1 furlong = 201.168 m
1 acre = 0.4047 hectares
1 sq km = 100 hectares
1 sq mile = 2.59 square km
1 ounce = 28.35 grams
1 pound = 0.4536 kilograms
1 short ton = 0.90718 metric ton
1 short ton = 2,000 pounds
1 long ton = 1.016 metric tons
1 long ton = 2,240 pounds
1 metric ton = 1,000 kilograms
1 quart = 0.94635 liters
1 US gallon = 3.7854 liters
1 Imperial gallon = 4.5459 liters
1 nautical mile = 1.852 km

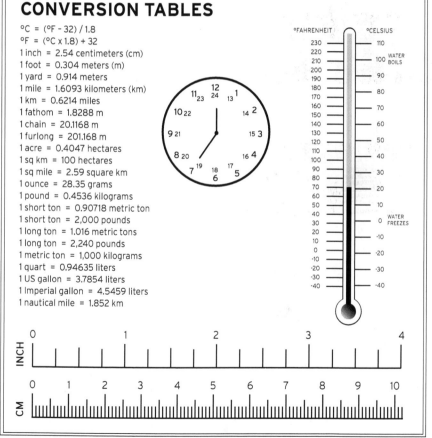

MOON SPOTLIGHT AUCKLAND
Avalon Travel
a member of the Perseus Books Group
1700 Fourth Street
Berkeley, CA 94710, USA
www.moon.com

Editor: Sabrina Young
Series Manager: Kathryn Ettinger
Copy Editor: Lisa Wolff
Production and Graphics Coordinator: Darren Alessi
Cover Designer: Kathryn Osgood
Map Editor: Kat Bennet
Cartographers: June Thammasnong, Chris Henrick, Kat Bennett
Proofreader: Natalie Mortensen

ISBN: 978-1-61238-494-8

Text © 2012 by Andrew Hempstead.
Maps © 2012 by Avalon Travel.
All rights reserved.

Front cover photo: Auckland skyline in late afternoon. # 8845494 © travellinglight / istockphoto.com
Title page photo: © Andrew Hempstead

Printed in the United States

All recommendations, including those for sights, activities, hotels, restaurants, and shops, are based on each author's individual judgment. We do not accept payment for inclusion in our travel guides, and our authors don't accept free goods or services in exchange for positive coverage.

Although every effort was made to ensure that the information was correct at the time of going to press, the author and publisher do not assume and hereby disclaim any liability to any party for any loss or damage caused by errors, omissions, or any potential travel disruption due to labor or financial difficulty, whether such errors or omissions result from negligence, accident, or any other cause.

KEEPING CURRENT

If you have a favorite gem you'd like to see included in the next edition, or see anything that needs updating, clarification, or correction, please drop us a line. Send your comments via email to feedback@moon.com, or use the address above.

ABOUT THE AUTHOR

© DIANNE MELTON

Andrew Hempstead

Australia native Andrew Hempstead may be cheering for the Aussies when it comes to cricket and rugby, but he has developed a deep appreciation for New Zealand and its people during a dozen or more trips to the country. He has traveled to New Zealand on assignment for the last four editions of *Moon New Zealand,* and to write and photograph for other publications, but many trips have been purely for pleasure – to kayak through the Bay of Islands and to ski the Southern Alps.

Since the early 1990s, Andrew has authored and updated more than 60 guidebooks, contributed to dozens of major magazines, supplied content for online clients such as Expedia and KLM, and been employed as a corporate writer for Parks Canada. His photography has appeared in a wide variety of media, ranging from international golf magazines to a Ripley's Believe it or Not! Museum. Andrew is an academy member of S. Pellegrino World's 50 Best Restaurants; he has spoken on guidebook writing to a national audience; and he has contributed to a university-level travel writing textbook.

Andrew and his wife Dianne own Summerthought Publishing, a regional publisher of nonfiction books. He and his family live in Banff, Alberta. His website, www.westerncanadatravel.com, showcases his work.